Readers React to *1623*

"I have been impressed by Robinson's work over the years and own a lot of his books. While *1623* is about New Hampshire, it deserves national attention. The Granite State has never had a more important history book. Damn good writing and thorough research. Wow, just wow!"
— *Fritz Wetherbee, NH storyteller*

"Robinson has written the best book ever on *1623* and the first English colonization of the New Hampshire coast!"
— *Richard M. Candee, Prof. Emeritus, Boston University*

"*1623* pulls back the curtain to expose long-held mistaken beliefs of what did and did not happen on the coast of what is now New Hampshire. Robinson's historiographical approach of contrasting multiple conflicting published accounts brings a new critical examination of old errors and even older myths to pick out the elusive truth."
— *Thomas M. Hardiman, Jr, Keeper and Executive Director, Portsmouth Athenaeum*

"A compelling narrative on New Hampshire's founder, *1623* reveals the all-but-forgotten life of David Thompson, his family, and their relationship to an island in the Boston Harbor."
— *Sylvia Watts McKinney, CEO & President, Thompson Island Outward Bound Education Center*

"Thank goodness for J. Dennis Robinson. While we've disposed of many grand myths of our past we still struggle with smaller ones that, in aggregate, form colorful but misleading narratives for the present. In **1623**, Robinson's dogged (and often controversial) pursuit of the facts seduces readers with ironclad ironies, secret scuttlebutt, and rigorously researched revelations that make our history all the more fantastic and entertaining."
— *Rick Broussard, editor emeritus of New Hampshire Magazine*

"**1623** is a masterpiece. It fits together details that my history friends and I have been puzzling over for decades."
— *Wendy Pirsig, Southern Maine historian*

"This important and entertaining read sets the record straight on New Hampshire's fascinating early history."
— *Emerson W. Baker, author of* A Storm of Witchcraft: The Salem Trials and the American Experience

"**1623** is a deep dive into what actually happened on the New Hampshire coast in its early years of European colonization. Robinson teases fact from fiction, setting the scene for the circumstances around David Thompson's settlement using the most up-to-date research. A must-read for anyone interested in the early history of New England."
— *Reagan B. Ruedig, NH historic preservationist*

1623

Pilgrims, Pipe Dreams, Politics
& the Founding of New Hampshire

Softcover ISBN: 978-1-7375736-4-7
Hardcover ISBN: 978-1-7375736-5-4

Library of Congress Control Number: 2023918939

Harbortown Press
Portsmouth, NH 03801

www.jdennisrobinson.com

Cover design: Harbortown Press
Cover photo: Joe Sohm, Dreamstime.com
Book production: Grace Peirce

To my dad
who at 100
is one-quarter the age
of New Hampshire

1623

Pilgrims, Pipe Dreams, Politics
& the Founding of New Hampshire

———— ◇ ————

By J. Dennis Robinson

Harbortown Press
Portsmouth, New Hampshire 03801

Contents

Acknowledgments

This book would not have been possible without the kind financial support of the following groups to which I am deeply grateful:

Seacoast Science Center, Rye, NH
Rye Historical Society
Strawbery Banke Museum, Portsmouth, NH
Music Hall, Portsmouth, NH
Portsmouth Historical Society
New Hampshire Society of Mayflower Descendants
Star Island Corporation
Isles of Shoals Historical & Research Association (ISHRA)
Piscataqua Savings Bank
New Castle Historical Society

As always, this manuscript was vetted by experts who offered hundreds of repairs, comments, and suggestions. The stellar team of beta readers this time included Thomas Hardiman, Terry Cowdrey, Wayne Bailey, Wendy Pirsig, Richard M. Candee, Kathryn Cowdrey, Peter Wiggin, and Nancy Hammond. My sincere thanks for their speedy yet careful editing. Kudos as always to co-designer and technical guru, Grace Peirce, who has been my guide through the rocky world of book publishing during two productive decades.

A Word about Words

While many documents use "Thomson" and "Tomson," I am sticking with the modern spelling of "Thompson" for our main characters. Apologies to purists, but spelling was fluid in the seventeenth century and there was no correct version. In a single legal contract, for example, Amias and David Thompson's first names were spelled half a dozen ways.

When referring to the English land grant for "Strawberry Bank," I prefer the standard spelling. That will distinguish the early colony from the ten-acre Strawbery Banke Museum that employs a nostalgic "ye olde" style spelling popular in the mid-twentieth century when the museum was created. I refer to Plymouth, England, as "Plymouth" and to the New England settlement as "New Plymouth" or "Plymouth Colony." The modern museum in Plymouth, Massachusetts, currently uses the spelling "Plimoth."

"Piscataqua" is used here for the river that separates modern New Hampshire and Maine. The region was called many similar things and, when relevant, I've indicated the spelling used by the early writer. "Pannaway" refers to the fortified house the Thompsons built in what is now Rye, New Hampshire.

Portions of this book are adapted from my earlier books on Strawbery Banke Museum, the Isles of Shoals, the town of New Castle, and from hundreds of my published articles about the region. There are no footnotes, by design, and no index. While this may frustrate historians, my primary goal here is to reach general readers who may be new to the topic with a straightforward narrative history. And while this is not intended as a scholarly work, I've done my homework, tons of it. Attribution to sources in the text should be found in an extensive bibliography. With luck, this work will generate further study by educators, students, genealogy fans, journalists, and professional historians.

INTRODUCTION

Turkeygate, an Introduction

By the summer of 1623, even the most courageous of the New Plymouth Pilgrims was distraught. Food was scarce. A supply ship from England to the "New World" was long overdue and feared wrecked at sea. Worse yet, according to Pilgrim leader Edward Winslow, "it pleased God, for our further chastisement, to send a great drought."

After six hot weeks, the half-grown ears of their meager corn crop hung dry and appeared dead on the stalk. Rows of stunted bean plants looked "as though they had been scorched before the fire." What had they done, the broken band of religious Separatists wondered, to incur such wrath from their God?

It is precisely at this point in the sorrowful story of New England's first permanent settlement that Mr. David Thompson stepped ashore at New Plymouth. He had come to save the day. At the request of Miles Standish, a military officer hired by the Plymouth Colony, Thompson arrived in the nick of time with a boatload of nutritious cod for the starving Pilgrims.

Although he earned but a single sentence in Winslow's writing, we learn Thompson was from a place called "Pascatoquack—where he liketh well." Thompson's newly established fishing and trading station, Winslow wrote, was about twenty-five leagues northeast of what would become Plymouth, Massachusetts. Thompson had built a fortified house at the mouth of the Piscataqua River, not far from the rocky Isles of Shoals. David, his wife Amias, their young son John, and a few unnamed English fishermen and servants became the first European immigrants to settle at what is now the tiny New Hampshire seacoast.

I stumbled onto this fact almost fifty years ago while rummaging among the shelves on the top floor of the University of New Hampshire library. I still remember the moment. It was 1975. I had already earned my degree in English Literature and was hanging around waiting for my girlfriend to graduate. I had been to England twice in the intervening years, but my imagined career as an author simply refused to launch, though not for want of trying. The refrigerator in my small Portsmouth, New Hampshire, apartment was plastered with rejection slips from some of the finest publications in the nation. I was surviving, meanwhile, as a substitute high school teacher during the day and delivering Domino's pizzas in my Volkswagen Beetle by night.

Why I was thumbing through Edward Winslow's *Good News from New England* (1624) is unclear. At the time, I had no thought of becoming a history writer and was determined to produce the next best-selling American novel. But a dozen history books and over 3,000 published history articles later, that award-winning novel still seems far away.

Back in 1975, I was looking for any story that I could sell to a magazine to pay for groceries. And this was a keeper. The idea that New Hampshire's first and largely forgotten English settlers had saved the legendary Pilgrims from starvation hit me hard. Why hadn't we studied this incident in school, or heard about David Thompson, or even New Hampshire's founding date of 1623?

It was the next passage in Winslow's journal that convinced me there was a story here. Thompson's codfish delivery to New Plymouth coincided with a soft sweet shower that broke the killing dry spell. Fourteen days of mild rain and moderate weather followed in 1623, reviving both the drooping corn stalks and the depressed Pilgrims. Only divine favor, Winslow believed, could bring "so great a change in so short a time." Thompson, like the rain, was a gift from God.

Where private prayer had not been sufficient, Winslow wrote, it was time for a lengthy communal "thanksgiving" service. "And therefore," he reported, "another solemn day was set apart and appointed for that end; wherein we returned glory, honor, and praise with all thankfulness to our good God, which dealt so graciously with us."

The annual family feast we've come to call Thanksgiving has little connection to the worshipful thanksgiving of 1621. The essay I wrote back then about the "second Thanksgiving," I admit, was provocative, irreverent, and downright silly. But I was young and hungry and slightly fed up with the sainted Pilgrims whose full story had not yet been fleshed out in revisionist history books like *Mayflower* by Nathaniel Philbrick. Back in 1975, we had just suffered through the Watergate affair and the resignation of President Richard Nixon. The Vietnam War was at an end. We needed to laugh again.

My short essay first appeared in 1976 as "Turkeygate: The Thanksgiving Scandal." I suggested that citizens of Massachusetts had been covering up the second Thanksgiving for almost 400 years. They had been hoarding the profits from Pilgrim-shaped candles, pumpkin pies, Butterball turkeys, and Thanksgiving TV-specials. I pictured Thompson as a kindly, well-educated, hard-working guy exploited by a cadre of religious zealots whose Puritan pals later tried and failed to wrest control of the eighteen-mile New Hampshire seacoast.

I demanded an apology from the entire Bay State and suggested Americans replace all stuffed Thanksgiving turkeys with fish chowder in honor of David Thompson. If not, the state of New Hampshire would seek revenge. We would continue to lure Massachusetts citizens across the border with cheap liquor and discount cigarettes, with outlet malls, lottery tickets, crystal blue lakes, ski resorts, and NO SALES TAX. I was kidding, folks—and young. But Turkeygate has been reprinted over the decades and was even read aloud one Thanksgiving on New Hampshire Public Radio.

In defense of my early satire, I believe Turkeygate has value. The key details in the article are true. The Pilgrims were an exclusionary group, almost forgotten by history until they were revived and rebranded in the 1800s. Half a century ago, my goal was to poke a few holes in the mythology of the *Mayflower* passengers. Today, even the leaders at Plimoth Patuxet Museums agree the Pilgrims did not embrace the concept of religious freedom, except perhaps, for themselves. Nor did they advocate for democracy, land at Plymouth Rock, live in harmony with indigenous people, or hold an event that in any way resembles a modern Thanksgiving dinner.

Yet even as we draw closer to the facts about New Plymouth, the story of David and Amias Thompson remains as mysterious as the Isles of Shoals on a foggy day. New Hampshire's founding family, it seems to me, is waiting to be revealed to twenty-first-century readers. That is my mission here.

When it suits us, New Hampshire boasts that its first Europeans "settled" here in 1623. Words carved into a large chunk of granite at the entrance to downtown Portsmouth make the same claim. But stop a few residents on the street and ask them who arrived here in 1623, where those settlers landed, why they came, and where they went? I expect you will get a lot of shrugs, blank faces, and misinformation. At this writing, even the local chambers of commerce, the official New Hampshire state website, Wikipedia, and countless history books and articles get the facts wrong. As the Granite State enters its fifth century, shouldn't we know what and who we are celebrating?

J. Dennis Robinson
2023

I. ARRIVAL

"To include the early inhabitants of New Hampshire with Puritans and among refugees from religious persecution, as some do, is to degrade to mere fable many of the best authenticated facts in history. The sole purpose of the first and of the subsequent proprietors was to acquire wealth by fishing and trading."

> — *Lorenzo Sabine,* Report on the Principal Fisheries of the American Seas, *1853*

"A glance at the map of New Hampshire would lead the uninitiated to conclude that the state, at one time or another, must have been awarded a corridor to the sea by Maine and Massachusetts."

> —*Elizabeth Forbes Morison and Elting E. Morison,* New Hampshire: A Bicentennial History, *1976*

"Our state history is not to any great extent in the popular mind."

> —*John Milton Winton,* Sketches of the History of New Hampshire, *1834*

CHAPTER 1
A Man with a Plan

New Hampshire's first European settler stepped ashore some-where between what is now the playground and the boat launch at Odiorne Point State Park in the town of Rye, New Hampshire. We don't know precisely where David Thompson built his fortified house, known to history as "Pannaway," but we're pretty sure he arrived at Little Harbor from Plymouth, England, on the merchant ship *Jonathan* by March of 1623.

Unlike the *Mayflower* Pilgrims who, three years earlier, were headed to the Hudson River, but ended up settling in Massachusetts, Thompson was not lost. He wasn't escaping from anyone or seeking religious freedom. His motivation was commercial. And he arrived, not in November at the onset of a brutal New England winter like his New Plymouth neighbors, but at the peak of the fishing season in the warming days of spring.

Although identified as a "Scotchman" in the Pilgrim journals, Thompson was likely from London and Plymouth, England. He was born in England around 1592, one century after Christopher Columbus reportedly "discovered America." Although New Hampshire history usually depicts him as a fisherman, Thompson was more accurately the manager of his Little Harbor fishery and fur trading post located roughly three miles from modern day Portsmouth, New Hampshire. Trained as an apothecary, he is variously referred to as a mariner, a gentleman, an attorney, an adventurer, an explorer, a clerk, an entrepreneur, a scholar, and a deputy governor of New England.

Thompson was well-connected to the powerful Sir Ferdinando Gorges, a naval and military commander who served as governor of the vital English port of Plymouth. Although Gorges never traveled to America, he worked tirelessly for four decades to plant a profitable New England colony that he intended to run much like a feudal lord. Land would be divided up among high-ranking owners who would rent it to hardworking tenants.

It was Gorges, along with Captain John Mason, who claimed ownership of what became the colonial provinces of Maine and New Hampshire. For his many attempts to send British settlers here, Gorges has been called "The Father of English Colonization in North America." And yet, he remains a shadowy figure even in local history. We will hear much more about Ferdinando and his son Robert Gorges as our story unfolds.

Odds are, David Thompson had carefully preselected his landing site at Little Harbor well before his "patent" was approved by the Council for New England late in the fall of 1622. In exchange for five years of labor in setting up a fishery, Thompson was to receive 6,000 acres of land and an island of his choosing. Those acres might have included a healthy chunk of the scenic Rye coastline plus the adjacent island town of New Castle. But Thompson ultimately selected an island in what would become Boston Harbor, where he was last seen alive a few years later.

How many times David Thompson explored the Atlantic coastline of the future United States, if at all, depends on who is telling the story. It has been suggested, without evidence, that a teenaged David was among over a hundred English men and boys who launched Popham Colony at the mouth of the Kennebec River in Maine in 1607. Not impossible, but not likely. Backed, in part, by Sir Ferdinando Gorges, the Popham crew constructed a fort and built a wooden ship, but they returned home the following year. Although much was learned about the Native Peoples and life in the New England wilderness, the 1607 Popham experiment in Maine was considered a failure. It briefly put a damper on northern colonization in what Europeans considered a harsh, cold, and savage region. All but lost to history, this early English attempt to get a foothold in what was then known as Northern Virginia was overshadowed by the successful Jamestown, Virginia, settlement well to the south that same year.

In their book *First Yankee* (1997) amateur genealogists Ralph and Matthew Thompson mixed facts with fascinating but unprovable theories about David Thompson. They imagined, for example, that Sir Ferdinando Gorges was grooming his young servant for big things by sending him on other transatlantic missions in 1616, 1619, and in 1621. That would mean Thompson, an apothecary with his own shop, had logged over 24,000 ocean miles in hair-raising trips aboard tiny wooden ships before deciding to bring his wife and young son here in 1623. Without the need for facts, all things are possible.

It is more credible that Thompson chose his destination through conversations with seasonal fishermen from Plymouth, England. He was undoubtedly familiar with Captain John Mason who, a few years later, planted the colony of Strawberry Bank (Portsmouth). Mason had spent years in what is now the Canadian Maritimes and may have personally toured the New England coast. Captain John Smith, who had mapped and named the New England region, was also in Plymouth, England, working for Gorges at the same time as Thompson. As the son-in-law of a prominent Plymouth shipwright, David certainly had access to the latest maritime news.

Whether David Thompson had been here before or not, in 1623 he made a beeline for Little Harbor at the mouth of the swirling Piscataqua River, and with good reason. Although he built his outpost on the mainland, Pannaway was barely seven miles by sea from the flat rocky Isles of Shoals. By the 1620s, these small islands were among the top staging spots on the Atlantic coast for splitting, salting, and drying codfish.

We know from the historical record that hundreds of English fishermen traveled annually to the fertile waters of the Gulf of Maine. We know from marine biologists that giant cod weighing well over 100 pounds flourished here in the seventeenth century. Recent archaeological digs at the Shoals have unearthed huge iron fish hooks and bits of Devonshire pottery left by fishermen as early as the 1620s. Settling at Little Harbor within view of the Isles of Shoals rather than further up the treacherous tides of the Piscataqua River, or further north in the frozen territory of Maine, was a wise choice for Thompson.

Thanks to Captain John Smith's game-changing book, *A Description of New England* (1616), everyone in Europe knew about the potentially profitable fishing grounds off Monhegan Island and the Isles of Shoals. But due, in part, to a Walt Disney cartoon, Smith is best known these days for his legendary link to the young Indian princess known as Pocahontas, whom he later claimed saved his life in Virginia.

It was after his Jamestown period that Smith explored this region and named it "New England." He extolled the rich bounty of fish, fowl, whales, wild game, fur-bearing animals, precious minerals, and tall trees just waiting to be harvested. Smith's book has been credited as starting the wave of English colonists, mostly Puritans, who used his famous map as their guide to the profitable American continent.

We know that John Smith made three failed attempts to return to New England to establish his own colony. Ferdinando Gorges was among his sponsors. But Smith's attempts were thwarted by bad weather, bad luck, and by French pirates. He spent the rest of his life in London. John Smith may well have planned to set up his fishery at or near the Isles of Shoals that he described as a heap of barren rocks. He named them "Smith Isles." In his famous book, Smith suggested, rather than funding two fishing trips annually, clever investors could increase profits by setting up permanent posts here. These men would overwinter along the coast, fishing and possibly trading with Natives, and be ready for the arrival of the spring fishing fleet. What John Smith only dreamed, David Thompson lived.

Barely four months after landing at present day Odiorne Point, with the Shoals on the seaward horizon, Thompson loaded his shallop with salted cod and headed south. Days later, New Hampshire's first English settler delivered his cargo to the starving Separatists at New Plymouth. Pilgrim father Edward Winslow mentioned Thompson as living "near Smith Isles (the Isles of Shoals) at a place called Pascatotquack."

In 1623 David Thompson was a man of great potential. He was an official agent of the Council for New England that handed out patents to land they didn't own and knew little about. Ferdinando Gorges, the Council president, had high hopes that Thompson would establish a profitable plantation. Thompson's three investors to whom he was indentured were hopeful too. But the Thompson adventure we celebrate as the founding of the "Live Free or Die" state, like the Strawberry Bank experiment that followed in 1630, would not go as planned.

CHAPTER 2
Aboard the *Jonathan*

When it comes to early American history, too many of us grew up with the "seven ship theory." First came Columbus in 1492 with his tiny *Nina, Pinta,* and *Santa Maria.* He landed among the Caribbean Islands, never saw the mainland and, thinking he was in India, called the natives Indians. Then, in 1607, the first permanent British settlement in North America was established at Jamestown, Virginia. Three little wooden ships named *Susan Constant, Godspeed,* and *Discovery* left 104 men and boys behind in Virginia. Only half of the first arrivals survived the first winter. And, of course, it was the famed *Mayflower* that delivered 102 founding citizens to a mythical Plymouth Rock in 1620. Half of those died within a year.

While naming the seven ships might help with a history quiz or crossword puzzle, they offer barely a glimpse of how the Eastern United States was born. They draw attention to two British colonies in 1607 and 1620 while ignoring the Dutch of New Netherland, who were settled near Albany, New York, in 1615 or the first French fort at Dochet Island in Maine in 1604. New Englanders often forget the first permanent Spanish settlement at St. Augustine, Florida, in 1565. European fishermen visited present day Newfoundland as early as 1540 and found their way to New England waters in the early 1600s, while Vikings had boots on the ground in Canada by 1000 A.D.

They all arrived by boat and few kept records. Historian David B. Quinn estimated that at least 650 European fishing and trading ships made the transatlantic journey to North America in little more than a century prior to 1612. Then the traffic increased.

Had it not carried the Pilgrims and become a superstar, the *Mayflower* would likely have remained a forgotten entry in some archived shipping log. Built around 1608, it was a typical European cargo ship. Before its only Atlantic crossing with its now famous passengers, the square-rigged 100-foot long *Mayflower* usually transported lumber, tar, and wine from European port to port. Its 180-ton rating tells us that the *Mayflower* could carry 180 casks (or "tunnes") of wine. The "*Jonathan* of Plymouth" by comparison was rated at 160 tons.

Before carrying Thompson to New Hampshire, it appears that the *Jonathan* delivered a sizable group of settlers to Jamestown in the summer of 1620. We have no image of the ship that also brought New Hampshire's founding family. But we can easily replace it with any picture of the Pilgrim ship we know so well. *Mayflower II*, a replica built in 1959, still sits in Plymouth Harbor, within view of the granite temple that encloses the legendary Plymouth Rock. The lines of the famous ship can be seen on countless magazine covers, postcards, tea towels, postage stamps, tote bags, models, medallions, coffee mugs, and just about everything else.

The little we know of the *Jonathan* comes from David Thompson's 1622 indenture to three Plymouth merchants—Abraham Colmer, Nicholas Sherwill, and Leonard Pomeroy. It appears that two of the investors owned *Jonathan*. The three men were risking a lot in backing Thompson. They were familiar with the dangerous, but often profitable, Atlantic fishing industry. They were likely inspired by accounts of Captain John Smith and others who claimed giant codfish practically leapt into their boats.

The three Plymouth sponsors agreed to provide Thompson and his small crew with "victuals, provisions, etc. as shall suffice them till they are landed." The cost of passage for Thompson's crew, seven men according to the indenture, was to be borne by all parties equally. Besides paying back Colmer, Sherwill, and Pomeroy from fishing profits, Thompson owed them one-quarter of all the land granted to him in America, assuming he completed his five-year indenture. It would prove to be a poor investment indeed.

The *Jonathan* had to carry all the tools and manufactured items Thompson and his men would need to build a fortified house and set up a fishery. That must have included a number of small fishing boats and a good-sized "shallop" or sailing ship. Taken apart and stored for the voyage, the shallop would be reassembled on the New Hampshire shoreline.

Whether Thompson's team suffered any of the discomfort and trauma endured by the *Mayflower* passengers is unknown. We have no record of their journey. But they were a much smaller band and, unlike the Separatists, these were probably professional fishermen familiar with the sea. Most were planning to return to England once their contracts were fulfilled, having earned a healthy profit and been granted a slice of New England real estate.

Colmer, Sherwill, and Pomeroy, who were among the successful fishing merchants of Plymouth, undoubtedly had bigger plans than dropping off Thompson and his people. It has been suggested that the *Jonathan*, by arriving in March or earlier, was among the many British fishing boats that were already anchoring each year off the Isles of Shoals where a seasonal crew dried their catch. It was risky and exhausting work, but a five or six month voyage could net a fisherman many times his annual income back home. The most dangerous part of the trip was getting past the French pirates that patrolled the waters around Great Britain. Having filled the hold of the *Jonathan* with tons of nutritious, flavorful, and valuable dried cod, the seasonal fishers set sail back to England, leaving Mr. Thompson to make his tiny mark in American history.

CHAPTER 3
Who Else Came Along?

According to David Thompson's contract with his investors from Plymouth, England, he could bring four men with him on the *Jonathan*. Three more men would follow at no specified time aboard the *Providence* for a full crew of seven. Our first problem here is that Thompson's indenture, signed with his investors on November 16, 1622, is only a promise of what was supposed to happen, rather than a record of what actually occurred. In December, Thompson asked the Council to allow passage for a total of ten people, but some historians suggest his additional request was ignored. Our second problem is that none of the passengers was named.

We know that Amias Cole Thompson, David's wife, lived with him at Pannaway, but how and exactly when she arrived is unknown. Born around 1597, married to David in 1613, Amias was the daughter of William Cole, a prominent Plymouth shipwright. An early document from 1615 shows the couple living in a large, newly-built, Plymouth apartment for ten shillings per year. Giving up that cozy home in England for a fishing outpost on an unsettled shore was a sacrifice indeed.

By 1623, the Thompsons had been married ten years. Amias may have been on the *Jonathan*. Or possibly David preceded his wife into the New England unknown in order to build their fortified house and set up his outpost. It also makes sense that, as a woman of significant social status in Plymouth, England, Amias was accompanied on the perilous journey by a female companion and servants.

Despite the lack of any record of her passage, that notion is strongly supported by a phrase buried in a report by Thompson's friend Samuel Maverick, an early Massachusetts colonist. In his *Description of New England*, published decades later in 1660, Maverick noted Thompson came from Plymouth "with a considerable company of servants." And Maverick should know. Spoiler alert: Within a few years of their arrival at Little Harbor, David would disappear and his widow would marry Samuel Maverick.

The Thompsons had three girls and a boy. Genealogical research suggests two of the girls, both named Ann, died at birth or in infancy in England in 1615 and 1620. Priscilla Thompson, the middle daughter born around 1616, appears to have survived. The adventurous couple left all three daughters in Plymouth. Two were in the graveyard and one, we assume, in the care of the Cole family. The Thompsons would never return. Only their son, John Thompson, made it into the New England historical record. Many accounts suggest John was born at Little Harbor, making him New Hampshire's first non-Native birth. But Plymouth church records prove otherwise. John was born in England in the county of Devon in 1619. This means John was about four when he arrived at Little Harbor. He will reappear in our story, long after his father's death, to claim an island in Boston Harbor.

Not having a clue who arrived with Thompson or who followed soon after has created another popular myth about New Hampshire's founding days. The confusion began in 1680 with Reverend William Hubbard's publication, *A General History of New England*. Hubbard wrote that a group of English investors called the Laconia Company sent Thompson to the Piscataqua River in 1623. But the Laconia Company, the investment group that later founded the settlement at Strawberry Bank, was not even formed until after Thompson's death in 1628.

"They sent over that year Mr. David Thomson [*sic*]," Hubbard reported, "with Mr. Edward Hilton and his brother, Mr. William Hilton, who had been fishmongers in London, with some others that came along with them." Hubbard guessed, without proof, that the Hiltons accompanied Thompson in 1623. Hubbard then assumed, again without evidence, that the brothers immediately set up a competing fishery just a few miles up the Piscataqua River at Hilton's Point on the outskirts of the town of Dover. Currently home to Hilton Park, the spot is also known as Dover Point.

Hubbard wrote the earliest account of the founding of New Hampshire. Later writers simply took him at his word. But Hubbard was writing more than half a century after 1623 in a world without newspapers or access to key provincial documents. Hubbard could not have examined the 1622 indenture of David Thompson, the document from the Council for New England, because it did not turn up for almost two centuries after Hubbard published his sketchy history.

Scholar Charles Deane, who discovered and studied the Thompson patent in 1876, argued convincingly that the Hilton brothers settled in Dover no earlier than 1628. "Historical facts seem often to have lain, in Hubbard's mind, in a loose and chaotic form," scholar Elwin Page wrote in 1922 prior to New Hampshire's 300th anniversary. "There is not a shred of proof that William and Edward Hilton came over with Thompson," Page concluded.

Reverend Jeremy Belknap, who lived for twenty years in Dover, published the first major history of New Hampshire in two volumes beginning in 1784. Belknap also had limited access to critical documents, so he took Hubbard at his word and repeated the imaginary Hilton narrative. Belknap, who is often quoted today, also incorrectly identified Thompson's investors, claimed he was from Scotland, and missed the date of Thompson's move to Boston by at least two critical years.

The theory that New Hampshire was settled in 1623 by two groups at the same time is without foundation or logic. And yet, it is recycled by local historians and disseminated in books, periodicals, and across the Internet. The state's origin story, as a result, is more baffling than it needs to be.

In the words of English dictionary writer Samuel Johnson, "Many things which are false are transferred from book to book, and gain credit in the world." Hubbard's unsupported claim caused a furor among local historians during a New Hampshire bicentennial in 1823. Later in this book we'll explore why the Hilton myth refuses to die.

It can be difficult for history writers to admit what we don't know, to hold back on theories, and to avoid connecting random dots. "It's easier to fool people," as Mark Twain pointed out, "than to convince them they've been fooled." Which may be why so much of early American history is not actually history, but stories we like to tell ourselves about a past that never happened.

Unless forgotten documents reappear, we do not know the names or the number of people from England who first settled on the New Hampshire shore. Historians are certain, however, that David Thompson was here in 1623.

We know this beyond doubt because at least six men independently reported this fact. Most of them were in the room with Thompson in his house at Little Harbor that very year. Exactly when Amias Thompson, her retinue, and her son John joined him at Pannaway can be debated until the cows come home. The correct answer, as with so much of the Thompson story, is simply —we do not know.

CHAPTER 4
The First Peoples

What we do not know about the dawnland days of the Piscataqua region and its inhabitants is mind-boggling. Most accounts of early Portsmouth barely mentioned its original occupants and archaeological evidence within the city limits is scarce. Educators have begun, at last, to reference Abenaki (or Wabanaki) "People of the Dawn." Public events now often begin with this acknowledgment: "We are on the homelands of the Abenaki people who have ongoing spiritual and cultural connections to this area." It is a starting point in a growing effort to come to grips with the way Europeans took over Native lands and destroyed or largely drove off its people. White Christian colonists proceeded to obliterate much indigenous history, leaving little beyond Native place-names, cultural stereotypes, and tales of Indian wars.

By the time the Thompsons made their brief appearance here, Native families had occupied the region for at least 12,000 years. New Hampshire lakes, rivers, woodlands, and mountains were once populated by indigenous people. They lived in a world with sophisticated legal, social, spiritual, agricultural, architectural, military, and technological ways—indeed every human system that could be found in European cultures.

Like David Thompson, Natives were drawn to the seacoast's abundance of fish, fowl, and shellfish. Since the last Ice Age, coastal Natives fished expertly from dugout and birchbark canoes using hooks and bone-tipped harpoons. They traveled far offshore. They caught cod,

14

swordfish, sharks, seals, porpoises, even small whales. Recent archaeological digs at the Isles of Shoals revealed stone tools and burned or
"calcined" fish bones dating back six thousand years.

Not long ago, a seacoast fisherman hauled in a strange item. It
turned out to be the fossilized tooth of a wooly mammoth, a hairy
elephant-like giant with curled fifteen-foot-long tusks. The mammoth
went extinct in North America 10,000 years ago. These creatures,
therefore, shared this region with indigenous hunters for at least two
thousand years.

And yet our New Hampshire founding story, drawn from the scattered reports of English explorers and settlers, includes few indigenous
tales. Bartholomew Gosnold, who explored the New England coast in
1602, was surprised to encounter eight Indians in a European-style
fishing shallop sailing off Cape Ann. One man in the Native group wore
"Christian" clothing, Gosnold reported, including a black waistcoat,
breeches, shoes, stockings, and a hat with a band. The other Natives
were naked except for short pants made from sealskin and deerskin.
The Indians gave a lengthy speech using some "Christian words" and
drew Gosnold a map of the area using a piece of chalk. In memory of
this initial close encounter with an obviously intelligent and adapt-
able race, Gosnold named the location of the meeting "Savage Rock."
Native Americans, despite their obvious sophistication, would remain
"savages" and "heathens" to many New England historians through the
next three centuries.

Martin Pring, who sailed up the Piscataqua River in 1603,
spotted no Natives, but "found signs of fires where they had been."
While visiting the Isles of Shoals in 1623, explorer Christopher Levett
declared, "Upon these islands are no savages at all." They had been
there, however, long long before the great pyramids rose above the
sands of Egypt.

Like the Plymouth Pilgrims, David Thompson appeared only a

few years after the Great Plague of 1616 to 1619. Historians suggest as many as eighty or ninety percent of some indigenous groups were almost wiped out by exposure to smallpox, yellow fever, and other diseases carried by Europeans. Where thousands had occupied the region a few years earlier, only hundreds remained. Piscataqua region Natives, those few who survived, were in no position to repel or even confront the tiny British fishing and trading post at Little Harbor.

English settlers saw opportunity amid the tragedy. "God had laid this country open for us," Captain John Smith wrote. "Where I had seen 100 or 200 people, there is scarce ten to be found." Pilgrim governor William Bradford offered a ghastly description of another wave of smallpox that struck Natives in 1633. "For it pleased God to visit these Indians with a great sickness," he wrote, "and such a mortality that of a thousand, above nine and a half hundred of them died, and many of them did rot above ground for want of burial." English settlers and the historians who followed frequently saw the devastation as a sign that God had prepared the way for them to dominate the region.

Nineteenth-century Portsmouth journalist Charles Brewster, like the leaders of New Plymouth before him, imagined seventeenth-century New England as a vast unpeopled territory ripe for the taking. "The noble Piscataqua," Brewster wrote, "was unvisited and unknown." Yet the original names of the Piscataqua River settlements are evidence that the Indians were nearby. Winnichahannat or Cochecho, for example, became the town of Dover. Squamscott became Exeter, Winnicunnet became Hampton, while Newichawannock evolved into South Berwick, Maine.

The popular theory that David Thompson got along favorably with the local Indians may be a modern invention. And while it has been suggested he personally negotiated with Natives during earlier visits to New England, this seductive rumor has yet to be proven. One contemporary reference hints that Thompson, at the very least, was a "gentleman" and a man of "good judgment" who got along well with everyone from scholars to travelers, and from the Pilgrims to the First Peoples.

This sentiment comes from Thomas Morton, a lawyer, colonist, and fur trader from Devon, England. He found the Massachusetts tribes fascinating. The subject of a future chapter, Morton set up an Indian trading post at what became Quincy, Massachusetts. His loosely run operation at "Merry Mount" was marked by maypole dancing, drinking, mixing with and selling guns to the Natives.

Morton was convinced, having visited Plymouth Colony in 1622, that the harsh, pious band of Separatists were exactly the wrong kind of people to establish a new nation in an already occupied land. Morton imagined a brave new world where the Algonquin people and European immigrants cohabited peacefully. Supported by Sir Ferdinando Gorges (who also backed David Thompson), Morton worked unsuccessfully to revoke the Pilgrim charter in the English courts.

In his *New England Canaan (1637),* Morton offered a rare glimpse into Native life. He described their day-to-day habits—moving seasonally, building durable homes, sleeping on plank beds draped with animal skins, and sharing their food and shelter with visitors.

"If you be hungry, there is meat for you, where, if you will eat, you may," he wrote of the Indians. "Such is their humanity."

Natives, Morton explained, wore clothing that suited the seasons. Their eyesight and sense of smell were remarkable. Their children were mannered and respectful of their elders. The Algonquins he knew from experience were honorable, their ability to heal was powerful, and their rituals deeply observed. For proposing the radical theory that Indians and the English could live in harmony, Morton was fined, jailed, and driven out of New England by Puritans.

As Dartmouth historian Jere R. Daniell pointed out in his book *Colonial New Hampshire*, our view of Native American life in the 1600s and beyond is "almost totally dependent on European reports and these are scarce and notoriously undependable."

As a case in point, John Milton Whiton argued in 1834 that the "aboriginal people" of the region "have disappeared from the earth." A Presbyterian minister, Whiton wrote *Sketches of the History of New Hampshire*. In his words: "The occasional exhumation of their bones, and the frequent discovery of arrowheads, stone pestles and hatchets turned up by the plow, are all that remind the present inhabitants of their ill-fated predecessors! Scarce an Indian now remains in the state." This was never true.

Whiton further argued New Hampshire Indians were never cheated out of their ancestral lands by English settlers. The transfer of hundreds of acres in exchange for a few trinkets, shirts, and kettles, he explained, was "fair and beneficial" to all parties. Whiton, for the record, also incorrectly reported details of the English settlements at Little Harbor and Strawberry Bank.

In his 1888 *History of New Hampshire*, published 265 years after the Thompsons arrived at Pannaway, John N. McClintock offered a patronizing view of the state's First Peoples. Indians were physically "splendid," honest, and hospitable, McClintock wrote. But they were "children of the forest" and "should have been treated as children or wards," he added. This to a people who had thrived in the region long before the days of "Cheddar Man," the oldest known human skeleton discovered in England.

In 1899, during the dedication of a tombstone-shaped memorial at Odiorne Point, the speaker praised David Thompson. The appearance of an Englishman brought "civilization" to the New Hampshire shore, the speaker announced, "before which aboriginal barbarism reluctantly withdrew."

Despite the movement to "decolonize" our view of the past and to include indigenous points of view in American history, the battle is far from won. In 2021, for example, former Pennsylvania senator Rick Santorum was dismissed from his job as a CNN commentator for allegedly making "dismissive" remarks about indigenous people.

"We birthed a nation from nothing," Santorum told a group of young political conservatives. "I mean, there was nothing here. I mean, yes, we have Native Americans, but candidly, there isn't much Native American culture in American culture."

CHAPTER 5
Building Pannaway

S ailing out of Plymouth Sound from England early in 1623 the *Jonathan* passed Rame Head, a promontory at the tip of a long Cornish peninsula. The shell of a stone chapel dedicated in 1397 still stands today. It was the last view of his homeland David Thompson would ever see.

Two months later, anchored at Little Harbor, his small team began construction of New Hampshire's first European-style shelter. A dense old-growth forest provided lumber, while the rocky shoreline offered stones for the foundation. The structure would naturally have been located at a high point, with the clearest view of the Piscataqua River "back channel." The faster and deeper main channel was in the distance, and the Isles of Shoals glimmered on the horizon.

As noted, historians have theorized David Thompson and a group of "fisherman-builders" from Plymouth, England, made an advance trip to the region from 1621 to 1622. Their assignment was to set up a fishing operation for Ferdinando Gorges at the Isles of Shoals. During a break between the fall and spring fishing seasons, Thompson was reportedly hired to oversee construction of Pannaway and return the following year.

This intriguing yet dubious thesis belongs to Ralph and Matthew Thompson, the two brothers from Oregon who became engrossed in the David Thompson story while researching their family history. Their dogged pre-Internet scholarship, mixed with wild flights of fancy, cannot be ignored, nor relied upon. David Thompson's 1622 indenture from the Council for New England, however, implies that no such advance trip occurred. The indenture instructs Thompson to select six thousand acres of land and to find "a fit place to settle and erect some houses or buildings for habitations, and to begin the same."

According to Samuel Maverick, who had certainly visited the site, "Mr. Thompson . . . built a strong and large home, enclosing it with a large and high palizado with mounted guns, and being stored extraordinarily with shot and ammunition was a terror to the Indians."

The "palizado" or defensive palisade of tall wooden stakes fixed in the ground was a common feature in early colonial forts. The Plymouth Pilgrims, too, mounted their fort and palisade with small cannon, as much a defense against invading French, Spanish, or English pirate forces as against an attack by Natives. Maverick would later do the same with Thompson's help at his house in Massachusetts.

The structure and outbuildings would have to accommodate three members of the Thompson family and their guests, plus servants and up to ten fishermen. The site was ideal for gardens and freshwater springs. There was a beach area for pulling small boats above the tide. A saltworks provided sea salt used to dry fish on wooden racks called "flakes." Salted cod could then be stored, traded, sold, or shipped back to Thompson's investors in Plymouth.

Other than Maverick's reliable account, which was not published until 1660, we have few aids when it comes to visualizing Pannaway. It has been suggested that "Pannaway" was simply another misspelling of the Abenaki term *pesce tegwe*, heard by English speakers as "piscataqua." It translates roughly as "branch of the fast flowing river." Others claim that the name, if it was used at all, came from its English builders.

We can once again thank Reverend William Hubbard, the esteemed minister of Ipswich, Massachusetts, for mixing up New Hampshire's founding story. Not only did Hubbard launch the myth of the 1623 Hilton settlement in Dover, but he seems to have conflated the Thompson house at Little Harbor with a later "Great House" upriver. Built in 1631 by Captain John Mason's settlers at Strawberry Bank, the Great House was a communal living structure. Hubbard incorrectly referred to Thompson's Little Harbor house as Mason Hall and claimed "the chimney, and some part of the stone wall is standing at this day." Hubbard was writing in 1680 when, evidence suggests, the ruins of the Great House on the Portsmouth waterfront, not Pannaway, were still visible. Other early writers have referred to Pannaway as the Manor House, Gorge's Fort, Thompson's Fort, Fort Pannaway, Rendezvous, and the Governor's House. And yet, its true design will remain a mystery.

A few historians, drawing from Hubbard, picked up the idea that Pannaway was built entirely of stone. Victorian researcher John Scribner Jenness, usually a reliable source, described the Thompson house as "laid upon a foundation of sea sand and small stones packed close into a trench." There was no cellar and the walls, he suggested, were of slate-like shale.

A stone house? Perhaps. The most common form of West County building was the "long house," Portsmouth historian Tom Hardiman explains. These were single-story stone structures with few, if any, windows and were only one-room wide. The long house had a single heated room in the front with one or more unheated rooms behind, and an attached "shippon" or barn. It would have been a grim, dark, and cold habitation for the Thompson team. The defensive guns would have been mounted at the surrounding palisade nearby. Without mortar, possibly pointed with clay, and set in wet beach sand, Hardiman says, the structure would not have lasted long.

Or equally possible, Pannaway had a stone foundation and chimney with hand hewn wooden walls. When it comes to picturing the scene at Little Harbor, everyone is guessing.

Jenness toured the supposed Pannaway site almost 250 years after the Thompsons had moved on. Jenness and countless tourists of his era visited while summering at New Castle nearby. Guests of the Wentworth Hotel across Little Harbor routinely hiked, rode horseback, or took a carriage ride a few miles along the scenic road in Rye to what they imagined were the ruins of New Hampshire's first European house.

John Albee, a New Castle poet, gentleman farmer, and friend of Jenness, made a pilgrimage to the hallowed site in the early 1880s. Albee wandered into an old cemetery where a human skeleton lay on the ground. Disgusted by the scene, Albee wrote:

> *So fares it with the Plymouth Rock of New Hampshire. The graves of its heroes neglected, their very bones laying about like broken crockery. And the relics of Mason's Hall consigned to a raisin box! Shame upon the state of New Hampshire! What has she ever done to preserve her early history?*

While Albee's criticism of New Hampshire has merit, there was certainly no trace of Pannaway to be found during his walks along the coast. The Odiorne family cemetery, however, can still be seen off the winding coastal Route 1A in Rye, between a small boat launch and the main entrance to Odiorne State Park. There you will find what may be the oldest marked graves in New Hampshire. The one-hundred-by-sixty-foot graveyard is surrounded by a sturdy stone wall and an iron gate.

The nearby farmhouse, barn, and cemetery are what's left of the Odiorne farm established in 1660. The family lived and worked here for 282 years, and the remnants of their tumbled structures were easily mistaken for relics of the Thompson era. At the outset of World War II, the federal government seized the Odiorne family's ancestral property by eminent domain, taking the land and homes of twenty-four neighbors. The 330-acre site, renamed Fort Dearborn, was transformed with huge artillery guns and underground cement bunkers, the remnants of which can be seen today. The military installation never saw any action and, despite efforts by former owners to reclaim their land, the waterfront acreage became a state park.

We can never know with any satisfaction when the Thompson team arrived or what Pannaway looked like during its brief heyday. But fragmentary reports written by early visitors offer tantalizing clues to what happened here. Explorer Christopher Levett, fisherman Phineas Pratt, Pilgrim enforcer Miles Standish, English profiteer Thomas Weston, and the first governor of New England, Robert Gorges, all took shelter at Pannaway. We'll check them out one by one following a quick trip back to England for the Thompson's origin story.

II. BACKSTORY

"The little that is known of Thompson's career excites a desire to ascertain what manner of man he was, and what, in its fullest bearings, was the purpose of his coming hither."

— *Frank W. Hackett*, Portsmouth, NH, lawyer and historian, *1886*

"No man will be a sailor who has contrivance enough to get himself into a jail; for being in a ship is being in a jail, with the chance of being drowned . . . A man in a jail has more room, better food, and commonly better company."

— *Dr. Samuel Johnson, British author, linguist, and lexicographer 1785*

"David Thompson was different from most of the adventurers of his day. He was a gentleman by birth, a trader, traveler and scholar."

— *Raymond W. Stanley*, The Four Thompsons of Boston Harbor, *1966*

CHAPTER 6
David, the Early Years

New Hampshire's first English settler was baptized on December 17, 1592 at St. James Church in Clerkenwell, a medieval parish of central London. The name "clerk's well" (a clerk was a learned person or clergyman) dates to 1100 AD. Once located outside London's ancient city wall, Clerkenwell was then known for its many brothels and populated by "dissolute, loose, and insolent people," according to a 1595 account.

William Shakespeare, an actor and budding playwright, was beginning to make a name for himself in London the year David was born. But the theaters were frequently closed due to deadly waves of the black plague. Clerkenwell would soon evolve into a fashionable seventeenth-century resort area with spas, theaters, and trendy homes. It has been known over the centuries for its breweries, printing shops, clockmaking, prisons, radical politics, and as home to London's "Little Italy." Today it is a diner's paradise of bistros, gastropubs, and bohemian brasseries.

Clerkenwell was also home to the well-respected Gorges family. Sir Ferdinando's father, Edward Gorges, lay buried in St. James churchyard. Ferdinando, the record shows, was living in Clerkenwell in 1590, the year his eldest son Robert was born. Decades later, Robert Gorges and David Thompson would hold a historic meeting at Pannaway in New Hampshire.

The theory that David Thompson was born in Scotland is widely circulated. Admittedly, two Pilgrim leaders called him a "Scotchman." A genealogical study, *The Thompson Family*, published in 1913, says the Norse surname (from "son of Thomas") was prevalent in Scotland. The first documented English use of Thompson, according to this study, was none other than David Thompson of Plymouth, England, who married "Amyas Colle" [sic] in 1613. In a 1995 essay published online, Genevieve Cora Fraser argued that the "real" David Thompson was from Corstorphine, Scotland, outside of Edinburgh. For our purposes and for most researchers today, the London baptismal records are convincing.

It makes sense that David's contemporaries detected a Scottish accent in a man raised in England by Scottish-born parents. We should also remember that King James I, who reigned over Great Britain from 1603 to 1625, had a Scottish accent. He was the son of Mary Queen of Scots. Mary was condemned to death by Queen Elizabeth and beheaded with three swings of the executioner's ax. James was eighteen months old in 1587 when he became King James VI of Scotland. The mature King James succeeded Queen Elizabeth, the woman who had killed his mother. He then became James I, King of England and Ireland.

The Pilgrims were not fans of James, who believed his "divine right" to rule came directly from God. The popular King James translation of the Christian Bible takes his name. And it was during the reign of James I that the *Mayflower* Separatists traveled 3,000 miles in a tiny wooden boat to escape his religious persecution.

So, just maybe, when the Pilgrim fathers made a point of labeling David Thompson in their published writings as a "Scotchman," they were sending a not-so-subliminal message. It would not have pleased the leaders of New Plymouth that Thompson was also a member of the Church of England, a lowly seller of fish, the leader of a competing trading post, and an agent of Sir Ferdinando Gorges and the Council for New England.

David appears to have been the youngest of five children born to

Richard and Florence (Cromlan) Thompson (Tomson). His parents were married at St. James in Clerkenwell, where David was baptized thirteen years later. He was about five when Martin Pring became the first European explorer to record a trip up the Piscataqua River in what would become New England. Pring was looking for sassafras that he called "a plant of sovereign virtue for the French Pox" or syphilis. Finding none along the Piscataqua, Pring sailed south.

Two years later in 1605, Samuel de Champlain "discovered" the Isles of Shoals where Natives had been hunting and fishing for thousands of years. Champlain is said to have landed at a place called "Cape of the Islands." Nineteenth-century historian Nathaniel Bouton, a clergyman and editor of New Hampshire's *Provincial Papers*, theorized that Champlain landed briefly at Little Harbor two decades before the Thompsons.

It has been suggested, without evidence, that David's father, Richard Thompson, served in the home of the Gorges family in Clerkenwell. If so, when Richard died in 1603, the same year as the death of Queen Elizabeth, his wife and youngest son may have kept a connection to the Gorges household.

"It is a temptation to try to make up stories about David Thompson's childhood escapades," Matthew Thompson wrote in *First Yankee*. And despite some extraordinary research, the author gave in to temptation often. The truth is, we have no further record of David until his marriage in 1613. And yet, *First Yankee* offers detailed descriptions of the boy's chores at Plymouth Fort and his wanderings around the city. When three kidnapped Native Americans were living in the Gorges household in 1605, *First Yankee* suggests young David Thompson became their English interpreter and guide. Such fanciful stories have frequently been taken as fact.

The final decades of the Elizabethan era were about exploring, plundering, and privateering rather than colonizing. David's childhood was filled with tales of swashbuckling sailors. Sir Francis Drake pirated Spanish gold, encircled the globe by sea, and defeated the Spanish Armada. Drake served as governor of Plymouth, as did the naval commander and slaver, Sir John Hawkins. So did the famed explorer, politician, poet, and spy, Sir Walter Raleigh. Raleigh is best remembered for his ruffled collars and promotion of tobacco. These colorful maritime characters, the superheroes of their day, inspired generations of young adventurers like David to risk their lives in search of foreign wealth, land, and power.

Drake, Hawkins, and Raleigh, like Sir Ferdinando, all served as governors of Plymouth. Their picaresque adventures were the pride of the city. But times were changing. The merchants of Sir Ferdinando's era were focused on the Newfoundland fisheries off the coast of modern Canada. Gold and easy riches were never far from their minds. Whether young Mr. Thompson grew up under the wing of Sir Ferdinando or not, the economic life of Plymouth had long been tied to the sea. And big rewards, for a man of David's modest social status, required big risks.

CHAPTER 7
When David Met Amias

New Hampshire's first settler was not a fisherman, but a pharmacist, a man trained to manufacture and sell medications. And while this is among the precious few facts we know about David Thompson, his career as an apothecary or apothecary's clerk is rarely mentioned. David worked in an age when doctors routinely bled patients until they passed out in order to remove impure fluids. Hemlock, arsenic, mercury, and deadly nightshade were frequently used as medications. David was on the job when the apothecary's manual, the *Pharmacopoeia Londinensis*, was published in 1618. Visitors to his shop may have seen and smelled shelves lined with decorative jars filled with herbs, teas, and potions familiar to modern holistic healers. There were also jars of blood, urine, sweat, animal fat and feces, shells, corals, insects, dried rhinoceros horn, powdered genitals, powdered Egyptian mummy, clay, fish, eggs, chemicals, nuts, roots, tree bark, berries, human fingernails, live worms, brains, bones, poisonous plants, minerals, mushrooms, mosses, hearts, and other curatives.

We know about David's career thanks to a document drafted by his father-in-law, William Cole (also spelled "Colle"), a Plymouth shipwright. Cole's daughter Amias appears to have been about sixteen when she married David Thompson in the parish church of St. Andrews in Plymouth on July 18, 1613. Dates vary, but the latest research suggests Amias was born "before October 3, 1597." She was probably the only child of Agnes Briant (Bryant) Cole, who died the following year in 1598.

Two years after the Thompson marriage, William Cole leased the young couple a comfortable apartment in a newly constructed building he owned. The "indenture" or deed was issued to "David Thompson of Plymouth aforesaid Apothecary & Ems his now wife." Spelling was fluid in the seventeenth century and Amias' name is elsewhere in the document spelled Amyis, Emes, Amyes, Amyas, and Amies, while David also appears as Davie and Davey plus Thomson and Tomson. This deed, a rare insight into the life of the Thompsons, was uncovered in the early twentieth century.

Their comfortable second-floor apartment included a kitchen, a shop for David's business, a "cottage," a hall, and two living chambers above the hall. William Cole lived in the same "tenement" that he built, apparently with money inherited from his late wife Agnes. The Thompsons owed Mr. Cole ten shillings "of lawful money of England." Their rent was due quarterly—upon the feasts of the Nativity of St. John the Baptist, St. Michael the Archangel, the Birth of the Lord God, and on the Annunciation of the Blessed Virgin Mary. The lease came with a lifetime guarantee unless the couple failed to make payments for a full year.

As we might expect, early records show ship owner William Cole did some work for Sir Ferdinando Gorges. We know a physician named Richard Vines also worked for Gorges, leading to speculation that it was Vines who guided David Thompson to his career as an apothecary. Maybe, maybe not. Richard Vines, for the record, was only about seven years older than Thompson.

Around 1616, Gorges sent Richard Vines on an exploratory voyage to spend the winter in the territory of Maine. Unable to find investors following the failed 1607 Popham Colony in the same region, Gorges grudgingly paid for the voyage out of his own pocket, plowing whatever profits ensued into future ventures. Vines successfully weathered the experiment at Winter Harbor, originally West Saco, Maine, and later named Biddeford. Maine historians have argued that the Biddeford colony was the first permanent New England settlement preceding New Plymouth.

Always eager to connect random dots, the *First Yankee* author suggested that David Thompson accompanied Vines on his Winter Harbor voyage. Thompson, it bears repeating, is never identified by name on any trip to the New World except to Little Harbor in 1623. Hiring his own boat, according to Gorges, "I got a Master and company for her, to which I sent Vines and others, my own servants with their provision for trade and discovery." Gorges had to pay his help an "extreme rate" to coerce them to spend the winter in Maine. Whether David Thompson, a professional apothecary with a wife and child, was among Gorges "servants" is unknown.

First Yankee delivers page after page of invented conversations between David and Dr. Vines, but doesn't stop there. Learning that the fabled Pocahontas was in Plymouth in 1616, *First Yankee* describes a meeting between Amias and the Powhatan princess. Married to John Rolfe of Jamestown, Pocahontas was known in England as Lady Rebecca Rolfe. The two women "got along famously," according to *First Yankee,* as Amias offered Pocahontas a tour of her apartment. They chatted about children, social customs, and, of course, they gossiped about Captain John Smith. These vivid flights of fancy have, unfortunately, made their way into genealogy websites as facts, further obscuring the truth about New Hampshire's first colonial couple.

Soon, back in England, Dr. Richard Vines married and had four children before returning to colonize the Biddeford region. His family received their patent in 1630 and survived many harsh New England seasons. But after an extended land dispute over territory with rival settlers, Richard Vines moved in 1645 to a plantation in the West Indies. A faded plaque at Biddeford Pool shows the English doctor visiting a Native village where the Almouchiquois people were in the throes of a deadly pandemic.

The year 1617, when Vines is believed to have returned from overwintering in Maine, was a historic time for pharmacists like David Thompson. From medieval days, apothecaries were in charge of places where wine, spices, and herbs were stored. From 1180 AD, these specialists were part of the Guild of Pepperers, best known for grinding things up with a mortar and pestle—still the symbol of your neighborhood pharmacy. Selling from their shops or from market stalls, apothecaries dealt with items "en gross," that is, groceries sold at wholesale prices. The pepperers, over time, evolved into the Livery of Grocers. But the apothecaries, who were experts in medicine, were unhappy being lumped in with "unskillful" grocers. King James I agreed, and in December 1617 he issued a royal charter creating The Worshipful Guild of Apothecaries based in London.

By the close of 1617, David and Amias had one living child, Priscilla, born soon after they settled into their Plymouth apartment. John Thompson, the couple's only son, was born in January 1619.

As the *Mayflower* Pilgrims faced their first killing winter, the Thompsons and their two surviving children were safely settled at home. As an apothecary in the port of Plymouth, England, David would have been a respectable man. His coat of arms from the newly formed apothecary guild showed Apollo, the god of healing, with his bow and arrow ready to slay the serpent of disease. Two mythical unicorns, favorite symbols of King James I, and a rhinoceros appear on the crest. The powder ground from their horns was considered a miracle cure. A Latin phrase on the apothecary coat of arms translates to "throughout the world I am called the bringer of help."

In less than two years, the Thompsons would exchange secure and promising lives for the perilous unknown, bringing along a young son and leaving a daughter behind. Why? For one, in America, David might become an extremely valuable man. Dr. Norman Gevitz, a medical historian, has identified only thirty-one apothecaries in New England's

first century. David Thompson appears at the top of that list, the first
of his profession to arrive here. Whether he practiced during his few
years in America is unknown. But in New France and in Virginia, Gevitz
noted, "early apothecaries investigated and reported on indigenous
plants and their supposed medicinal values."

We should keep in mind that healing plants and potions were
big business in the seventeenth century. Martin Pring and others had
made the transatlantic journey primarily to harvest sassafras in this
very region. America was widely known to have a "medicinal nature,"
and the search for new healing and stimulating plants was on.

Perhaps David Thompson's voyage to New Hampshire was both
commercial and humanitarian. He lived in an age of rampant disease
and infant mortality where two of his four children died soon after
birth. Beyond selling drugs, apothecaries also examined patients,
diagnosed maladies, and prescribed remedies. By 1620, David was
approaching his thirtieth birthday when the average life expectancy in
England for men was thirty-five. If he was going to make a difference,
the time had come.

CHAPTER 8
The Gorges Connection

To understand how David Thompson got here and how New Hampshire started, we must spend a few more minutes with Sir Ferdinando Gorges (c. 1567-1647). That's not easy because his first name is distracting. Although then common in England, "Ferdinando" sounds more Italian, Spanish, or Portuguese than the first name of a powerful Englishman who helped launch a dozen settlements from Maine to Massachusetts. But the Gorges family had deep English roots going back centuries, and Ferdinando inherited his name from an uncle. Today, books that offer baby names for expectant parents suggest Ferdinando means "adventurer" in Italian and "brave traveler" in German. Both are surprisingly on target.

Proud and aristocratic, the Gorges family kept a house in Clerkenwell, England, where Ferdinando's father Edward died in 1568 at age thirty-one. Edward was buried at St. James Church, where, readers will recall, David Thompson was later baptized.

Ferdinando was an infant when his father died. He inherited a gold watch, 100 pounds sterling, and a manor house. The next time we see Ferdinando in the historical record, he is about twenty-one years old. He has been wounded fighting in seemingly endless wars against Spain and France. By 1596, he was governor of the fort at Plymouth Harbor, a key coastal defense against Spanish attack. A friend of Robert Devereux, the Earl of Essex, Ferdinando got into hot water when Essex mounted an unsuccessful revolt against an aging Queen Elizabeth in

1601. Essex was beheaded, but Ferdinando, after being jailed and fined, was restored to his Plymouth post by King James I.

By 1605, the Spanish war was on hold and Ferdinando had a new passion. That year, explorer George Weymouth (also Waymouth) arrived at Plymouth, England, from an early visit to America. Weymouth had failed to find the legendary Northwest Passage, the imagined trade route to the riches of the Orient explorers had been searching for since Columbus. Spoiler alert: that same dream was instrumental in the settlement of Strawberry Bank, now Portsmouth, New Hampshire, in 1630. We'll discuss that popular misconception in a future chapter about the Laconia Company.

The English had been slow to colonize North America since a settlement at Roanoke Island, off the coast of modern North Carolina, failed in 1590. Over 100 colonists left behind by Sir Walter Raleigh simply disappeared. But George Weymouth was eager to try again.

Like those before him, Weymouth documented the bounty of Northern Virginia in what would be known as the territory of Maine. The region was rich with fish, fowl, plants, rivers, timber—all waiting to be exploited by English settlers. Weymouth also brought back five Abenaki Indians he had abducted. (They are named in English records as Amóret, Tahánedo, Manedo, Skicowáros, and Sassacomoit.) James Rosier, who joined and wrote about the Weymouth voyage, left this description of the abduction:

> We used little delay, but suddenly laid hands upon them. And it was as much as five or six of us could do to get them. . . . For they were strong and so strong as our best hold was by their long hair on their heads.

Three of the captives were presented to Gorges and lived in his household at the Plymouth fort for the next two years. Gorges said he found the Natives highly intelligent and civilized. They were, he wrote, "far from the rudeness of our common people."

It is here that Gorges "caught the colonization fever," wrote University of New Hampshire history professor Charles E. Clark. "From that moment until he died forty-two years later, Gorges' life was dominated by a single passion: to sponsor colonies in the place described to him in broken English by his homesick captives."

According to a letter written by Gorges, one of the kidnapped Indians in his care was Tisquantum, the true name of the legendary figure from Patuxet called "Squanto," who later served as a translator to the Pilgrims of Plymouth Colony. *First Yankee* author Ralph Thompson took a giant leap by suggesting it was young David Thompson who taught Squanto to speak English. It's a lovely story, but pure fiction. Even if Thompson happened to be in the Gorges' residence at the time, Squanto was not.

David Ring Adam, managing editor of *American Indian* magazine, explained why the popular legend is false. In his essay "Alien Abduction: How the Abenaki Discovered England," Ring says Tisquantum was from Patuxet village, now Plymouth, Massachusetts. Weymouth's kidnapped Indians were eastern Abenaki who lived 200 miles away in the tribal region centered near Bangor, Maine. Gorges' biographer, James Phinney Baxter, was convinced that Ferdinando, or a later editor of his private correspondence, simply got the name wrong. But a good myth is hard to kill and the connection between Thompson and Squanto is still repeated.

The entire English nation was fascinated by Gorges' three indigenous prisoners and two others hosted by Lord Chief Justice Sir John Popham of Somerset, England. (His nephew, Sir George Popham, is about to become a key character in our story.) Much more than curiosities, the Indians were potential translators for future exploration and might know the whereabouts of riches waiting to be tapped by the English. They were, Gorges later wrote, the inspiration for all his efforts to colonize New England.

American students learn how England planted its first permanent colony at Jamestown in 1607. But they rarely learn how "Virginia" then stretched north to the modern border of Canada. And while the London Company was settling Jamestown in Southern Virginia, a second group of investors authorized by King James I was planting a parallel colony at the Kennebec River in Northern Virginia, now Maine. Sir Ferdinando Gorges was deeply interested in this experiment authorized by the privately run Plymouth Company.

Led by George Popham, a British customs officer and friend of Gorges, 120 English men and boys, plus Skicowáros, left Plymouth, England, in 1607 aboard the ships *Gift of God* and *Mary and John*. Crossing the wide Atlantic, they set up operations at Sagadahoc, at the mouth of the Kennebec River.

Again, there is no evidence that a teenaged David Thompson was among the Popham colonists. Despite a bitter winter, they managed to build a fort armed with a dozen cannons. The men constructed a storehouse, a church, and fifty dwellings. The Popham colonists established trade with indigenous locals. Astonishingly, they also constructed a seagoing wooden vessel christened *Virginia*, the first English ship built in North America.

George Popham's risky commercial venture was also driven by a missionary zeal. Popham was tasked with propagating the Christian religion "to such people as yet live in the darkness and miserable ignorance of the true knowledge and worship of God, and may in time bring the infidels and savages living in those parts to human civility and to a settled and quiet government." The King James version of the Bible was even then being created by a panel of forty-seven translators and scholars to be published in 1611.

But George Popham, a harsh and honest leader with "an unwieldy body," died while in America. Within fourteen months, Popham Colony was abandoned, and with it went Sir Ferdinando's initial hope for a profitable settlement in Northern Virginia. Gorges' "grief and discontent were great" according to his biographer Baxter, when the members of the failed colony at Sagadahoc returned to England. Some arrived aboard the *Virginia*, their ship built in the New World. "All of our former hopes were frozen to death," Gorges wrote to a friend. It was but the first of many disappointments to come.

Although financially and politically damaged by his role in the Essex Rebellion against Queen Elizabeth, Gorges refused to give up his dream of striking it rich in America. His plan for governing the expansive territory, sometimes called a "palatinate," was to establish "lords of the land" much like a medieval kingdom. Each landlord would retain permanent ownership of his entire territory. He could then collect annual rents from residents who worked or lived on the landlord's property. With New France (Canada) to the north and New Spain dominating much of North America to the south and west, Gorges and other adventurers were eager to get boots on the ground. But King James had other interests. "The weak monarch," according to historian Baxter, "was more interested in getting a hawk or flying squirrel from the New World than in colonizing it." Exactly who called James "the wisest fool in Christendom" is unclear, but he was known to be both learned and impractical.

Pushed by the London Company investors, meanwhile, colonists flooded into Jamestown, Virginia, in the coming years. Hundreds of them died from starvation, disease, and Indian reprisals. Scholars now dismiss the legend in which an eleven-year-old princess Pocahontas (her real name was Amonute) saved the life of twenty-seven-year-old adventurer John Smith. By 1609, having left Jamestown, Captain Smith was back in England. By 1614, he was in North America again, this time hunting for whales and gold mines in the region he dubbed "New England." Smith found no gold and could not catch a whale, but he discovered the rich fishing grounds in the Gulf of Maine.

Smith was scarcely off the boat back in Plymouth, England, when he met with his "honorable friend," Sir Ferdinando Gorges. The two men planned Smith's return trip to set up an American plantation. "Could I have but means to transport a colony, I would rather live here," Smith wrote of New England.

With Gorges' encouragement, Smith made three attempts to start that New England colony. Was he headed to "Smith Isles," his name for the Isles of Shoals off the coast of New Hampshire and Maine? We'll never know. Smith's every effort was thwarted. His first ship turned back to Plymouth Harbor due to a broken mast. His next voyage met ferocious weather. He was captured by pirates and thrown into a French prison. A final voyage was called off after three months of contrary winds. Gorges lost interest in the unlucky John Smith and turned his attention to other adventurers.

But it was Captain Smith, ironically, who got Gorges back on track. Smith's bestselling book, *A Description of New England* (1616), not only gave the region its name, but turned the tide on public, political, and investor interest. Despite the failed Popham Colony in 1607, New England was looking attractive again. Aware that moneylenders were seeking a quick return, Smith mentioned the possibility of finding precious metals, pearls, and jewels in New England. He focused his sales pitch, however, on the smarter long game of tapping the unimaginable wealth from the region's natural resources.

Beyond the bottomless harvest from the sea, Smith wrote about fur-bearing animals, wild game, fruit trees, potash, timber for shipbuilding, clear fields, fertile black soil, thick grass, pitch tar, and salt marshes. There was the promise of planting vineyards, crops of corn, tobacco, cotton, hemp, herbs, and medicinal plants. A smart English investor, Smith calculated, might double his income with a five-month round-trip voyage. Two trips per year meant a 400-percent increase in profits, he projected. Smith also imagined the economic benefits of enslaving the region's indigenous people as a source of cheap labor.

Gorges had not been so excited about his chances for launching a New England colony since the arrival of the Weymouth Indians. After sending Dr. Richard Vines to test the feasibility of surviving the winters at Biddeford, Maine, Gorges dispatched two more exploratory ships. One was sent to confirm Smith's report of the incredible fishing off Monhegan Island, but that captain suffered from illness. Gorges sent a followup cruise under Captain Thomas Dermer, an explorer, navigator, and former associate of John Smith. Here again, with no proof, Thompson's biographers claim he was aboard during Captain Dermer's journey to the Isles of Shoals. But Dermer, weakened by disease and attacked by Natives, died at Jamestown in 1620.

Another 1,200 adventurous settlers had by now found their way to Jamestown, more than doubling the population. Tobacco profits, at first, were soaring. A new Virginia government was forming. And the first enslaved Africans had been forced onto the auction block. The London Company's Jamestown investment was paying off, while Sir Ferdinando's Plymouth Company had yet to create a single permanent colonist.

In August 1620, as the Pilgrims organized their exodus to a strange and frightening new home, Sir Ferdinando's wife Ann died. Three months later, as the *Mayflower* reached the coast of Cape Cod, King James finally decided it was time to colonize America. Gorges was ready to try again, and David Thompson was next in line.

CHAPTER 9
Other People's Money

It was good to be the governor of Plymouth, but it was not lucrative. While previous Plymouth governors had taken to politics, privateering, and piracy to build their fortunes, Sir Ferdinando imagined clusters of profitable American plantations supplementing his income. Each would send back a steady trickle of taxes and rental fees. So far, his Plymouth Company had come up empty, but following the advice of John Smith, Gorges would play the long game.

Behind every early English effort to colonize America, even New Plymouth, there was a room full of rich and powerful sponsors hoping to become richer and more powerful. By 1620, King James had come around to the idea that, without immediate effort, North America might be lost to the French, Dutch, and Spanish interests already in play. England also needed to protect its fishing rights along the fertile New England coast. Lacking the funds to do the work, the king signed off on a private group known as The Council Established at Plymouth in the County of Devon for the Planting, Ruling, and Governing of New England in America. The name says it all.

The Council included forty "noblemen, knights, and gentlemen" and at least two titled women. Sir Ferdinando Gorges, having already spent fifteen years attempting to establish a colony, was the natural leader. Early members included Raleigh Gilbert, who had been part of the Popham Colony in 1607. George Villiers, the controversial Duke of Buckingham, would later be assassinated while staying with Captain

John Mason at his home in Portsmouth, England. Henry Wriothesley, better known as the Earl of Southampton, was the dedicatee of two of William Shakespeare's poems. Famed art collector Thomas Howland, Earl of Arundel, we'll later discover, would receive the only known letter sent from America by David Thompson.

Members of both the House of Lords and House of Commons, as well as investors from English guilds, were included in the Council. Many of their names now appear on a map of New Hampshire and Maine, including Pembroke, Strafford, Bath, Exeter, Marlborough, Rockingham, Conway, Rochester, Sutton, Sandwich, Orford, Holderness, Mason, and Richmond.

For a modest investment, Council members were promised, not only a financial return, but "perpetual succession" of whatever towns and counties might be set up. In other words, their descendants would profit forever. Members of John Mason's family would battle for their slice of the New Hampshire pie right up to the American Revolution.

Council members had no way of knowing what vast territory lay beyond the New England coast. On paper, they were assigned to settle and manage all lands, rivers, and lakes lying between the 40th and 48th degrees of north latitude. In 1620, New England theoretically included what would become all land from modern Nova Scotia to Philadelphia and North Carolina, stretching across the continent to the Pacific Ocean.

Poorly organized and underfunded from the start, the Council relied on the small entry fee due from each of its forty members. There would soon be plenty of income pouring in, they incorrectly assumed, from selling fish, from selling fishing licenses, from merchant partners, from the fur trade, from land rental fees, and much more.

Colonizing a distant nation already occupied was daunting enough, but there was further resistance at home. English fishermen and their backers were opposed to the Council's attempts to control the entire Atlantic trade. The Council, with its royal charter, was seen by many as an unfair monopoly supported by an unpopular monarch. A lavish spender who enacted new taxes, King James was also a Scotsman who surrounded himself with favorites like the unctuous Duke of Buckingham. When the king ran afoul of Parliament, which was often, he simply shut it down and tried to run the government on his own.

The Council had other problems. Few of its members shared Sir Ferdinando's zeal for peopling New England. It was difficult to gather enough of them at a meeting to hold a quorum. Some never got around to paying their membership fees, leaving the group's finances perpetually in the red. That left their patentees dependent on private investors who, unwilling to play the long game, demanded quick profits. The Council also tended to issue vaguely defined and sometimes overlapping land grants.

With so many problems, it is surprising the Council managed to issue the few patents we know. The first, curiously, went in 1621 to John Pierce (or Peirce), a cloth worker from London. Pierce represented the Pilgrims of New Plymouth who, having initially planned to settle along the Hudson River, had no royal authority to be in New England. The Council granted Pierce 100 acres of land per settler and 1,500 acres for public use. New Plymouth, in return, owed the Council an annual rent of two shillings per 100 acres. This was on top of what they owed seventy merchant adventurers from London for their voyage aboard the *Mayflower*. That original deal was brokered by Thomas Weston, a London ironmonger who, we shall soon see, founded the doomed colony of Wessagusset. Weston also took shelter at Pannaway after being shipwrecked and stripped of his clothing by local Natives.

The Council was busy in 1622 with eight grants, including the indenture to David Thompson. Robert Gorges, son of Ferdinando and the subject of a future chapter, received a patent for Massachusetts.

This year Sir Ferdinando and Captain John Mason granted themselves all the coastal land between the modern Merrimack and the Kennebec rivers. They made no attempt to establish a colony at that time.

The 1622 Gorges-Mason patent bewildered New Hampshire's earliest historians who didn't know whether the owners had acted upon the grant or not. Years later, William Hubbard and Jeremy Belknap confused the Thompson outpost (1623) with Mason's later outpost at Strawberry Bank (1630). Even though the error was corrected in the late 1800s, historians who rely on Hubbard and Belknap today continue to foul up the facts.

Before it broke up in 1635, the Council for New England issued at least twenty-four patents to lands already occupied by indigenous groups. We are tempted, from a twenty-first-century perspective, to see the colonization of New England simply as an assault by greedy capitalists and religious zealots. But there were deeper motives. Gorges, for example, saw New England as the ideal place for his beloved nation, then overpopulated by the poor, to reduce its social problems by offering a new start to its poor and starving people. The Council and later efforts by Gorges also remind us there was, if only briefly, an organized movement to launch a very different New England than the Puritan stronghold it became.

In their defense, early English investors were playing a high stakes game. While seasonal fishing trips could be lucrative, landed settlements in New England routinely failed. Colonies at Sagadahoc, Monhegan, Cape Ann, Wessagusset and others would quickly collapse or become unprofitable. Future expensive efforts by Ferdinando Gorges, John Mason, and John Smith were also doomed, often before they left the harbor in England.

The London adventurers who bankrolled the *Mayflower* trip, historian Ruth A. McIntyre points out, "have often been described as hardhearted profiteers" who victimized the Pilgrims. Amid every hardship imaginable, it would take the New Plymouth colonists twenty-six years to pay off their debts.

Most of this risky business was as yet unknown to Abraham Colmer, Nicholas Sherwill, and Leonard Pomeroy, the English merchants who paid to equip the *Jonathan* for a local apothecary in 1622. All three men would serve as Lord Mayor of Plymouth. David Thompson's name flits in and out of early Council records where he appears to have performed clerical and administrative work. He was certainly known by the investors for his connection to Sir Ferdinando and to his father-in-law, Captain William Cole. But to date, scholars have not determined why these wealthy city leaders came to entrust Thompson with their high-priced gamble.

CHAPTER 10
In Cod We Trust

Fishing was to the founding of New England what harvesting tobacco was to Virginia. Profits from both cash crops encouraged English investors to invest and settlers to settle. David Thompson was only doing a high-tech version of what skilled indigenous fishers had done for millennia when Natives worked from dugout canoes.

How far back Europeans journeyed to the rich fishing grounds of North America is unknown. Legends claim the mysterious Basque people, who lived along the borders of France and Spain, secretly fished on the North Atlantic before the days of Christopher Columbus. They were possibly at work along the Grand Banks off Labrador and Newfoundland as early as the 1540s.

John Smith's vivid account of his 1614 voyage to New England is frequently credited with inspiring the English fishing boom. But his was not the first propaganda campaign. Captain Charles Leigh, while fishing for cod in the Gulf of St. Lawrence, had previously reported, "In little more than an hour we caught with four hooks two hundred and fifty." According to Leigh's 1597 account, codfish leapt from the sea directly into fishermen's wicker baskets. Cod were so numerous that in 1602 one fisherman recorded tossing them back because his boat was overloaded and in danger of capsizing. Explorers named Cabot, Cartier, and Champlain filed similar glowing reports.

By Smith's report, the prime fishing grounds of Europe were in sharp decline. Catholicism, meanwhile, was on the rise, requiring more and more people to abstain from eating meat during frequent holy days. Meat, as Brian Fagan explains in his book *Fish on Friday* (2007), was associated with carnal desires, while fish, a popular Christian symbol, was connected to purification, fasting, and atonement.

Following Smith's *Description of New England* in 1616, the race was on. Four years later, Sir Richard Whitbourne of Devon published a glowing treatise on the advantages of cod fishing and colonization in Nova Scotia. The industry, Whitbourne pointed out, was essential to the West Coast economy in England. It supported not only fishing families, but the builders of ships, the makers of nets, rope, barrels and hooks, plus bakers, brewers, merchants, and countless others. With the larger French fishery also busy in Canadian waters, the British were moving southward to Maine and the tiny Isles of Shoals.

It is worth noting that another early governor of a Newfoundland fishing operation was Captain John Mason, later a resident of Portsmouth, England. This is the same Mason of the Laconia Company who founded Strawberry Bank. Like Whitbourne, Mason published an enthusiastic report. In Canada, he saw "salmon and cod so thick by the shore that we hardly have been able to row a boat through them." In thirty days his men were able to kill, dress, and dry 25,000 to 30,000 fish, he boasted.

In 1622, as the Thompsons were planning their journey, the island of Damariscove in Maine—a site supported by Ferdinando Gorges and long popular with seasonal fishermen—housed thirteen year-round workers. They lived in a structure that, like Pannaway, was surrounded by a palisade of ten-foot-tall logs. A 1622 eyewitness described their defenses as "small shot, one piece of ordnance, and some ten good dogs." At least forty English vessels were working in the region that year.

Like Damariscove, the Isles of Shoals was an ideal staging site for processing dried cod known as "stockfish." The product was then shipped back to the ravenous European market. Dried cod was not only long lasting, but delicious compared to wet pickled and salted fare. Samuel Maverick, who seems to have known David Thompson well, described the Isles of Shoals in 1660 as "one of the best places for fishing in the land." David Van Deventer, a modern expert on seventeenth-century New Hampshire, says the Shoals "though rock-strewn and barren," provided the necessary warm and sunny weather for drying and cutting haddock and codfish.

As many as 600 men, mostly living aboard ships, worked at what can only be called island factories on Smuttynose, Hog (Appledore), and Star islands. Some fished in teams from small shallops, hooking 200 to 300 large fish per man per day. Paid per catch, British fishermen could earn three times their annual salary by making the long trip to America. Each man kept track of his catch by cutting out the fish tongues and impaling them on metal spikes.

While some men worked their boats at sea, crews known as "dressers" processed the catch. Back at Smuttynose Cove and standing in a row, assembly-line fashion, the skilled dressers performed the same task over and over. The "throater" cut the cod from belly to anus and passed it to the "header" who, after ripping out the entrails, tossed the liver into one basket and the roe into another. He neatly sliced off the head of the fish and kicked it into the sea through a hole in the staging platform. The "splitter" then separated the fish flesh from the backbone with lightning-fast movements of his sharp knife. Then the fish were dried, turned, and salted on rocks or wooden platforms called "flakes."

Like Damariscove, the Shoals were situated close to the mainland, offering a safer harbor than the open seas of the Grand Banks. With dozens of ships hovering around each staging site, Thompson's outpost at Pannaway was the next evolutionary step in building a permanent and profitable business on the mainland. Newly rich fish factory owners bought land. What appears to be innovative from a New England perspective, was in fact, the final stage of a centuries-long migratory journey for European fishers.

Up to 400 ships worked the region between Cape Ann and Monhegan Island by the time Thompson reached Little Harbor. Fifty or more came from Plymouth, England, including those owned by David Thompson's sponsors. Having filled their quota, the seasonal ships packed up and sailed home to market, especially to Spain, where profits were highest. Because fishermen liked to keep their prized spots secret and were often illiterate, historians had little hard evidence of the Shoals operation until modern archaeological digs.

Emmanuel Altham, captain of the English ship *Little James*, spent much of 1623 in New England. He was among the merchants who financed the Pilgrim experiment. Writing home to his brother, Altham described the fishing as "beyond belief." Any man who could finance a journey would easily double his investment, Altham predicted. He was skeptical, however, that the Pilgrims could succeed in the industry. "How is it possible that those men that never saw fishing in their lives should raise profit by fishing?" he wrote. Unequipped for full-scale fishing himself, Altham could load only a thousand cod on his return voyage. His men then caught 300 more for sport, some weighing 100 pounds, before tossing them back into the sea. Evidence suggests Emmanuel Altham also stopped at Pannaway in his travels since, in his will, he left forty shillings to a "mistress Thompson in New England" for repayment of a debt to her late husband.

While a handful of English arrivals were searching for God, thousands more were looking for cod. New Hampshire's founders were also on the lookout for copper, silver, gold, furs, gems, medicinal plants, and a secret passage to the Orient.

CHAPTER 11
Putting It on Paper

It took 250 years for American scholars to get the Thompson memo. A decade after the Civil War, the president of the venerable if not stuffy Massachusetts Historical Society handed an old parchment deed to Charles Deane. It was a revelation. Unimpeachably honest, Deane was a businessman from Maine with a passion for fact-based history. He had already studied the Pilgrim journals and the rare documents of the Council for New England. Suddenly, Deane found himself holding the lost indenture of David Thompson dated November 16, 1622.

No previous historian who wrote about the founding of New Hampshire, including Hubbard and Belknap, had seen this document. Here was Thompson's own copy of the contract, spelling out his legal arrangement with three Plymouth investors, their official seals still attached. It revealed the story of his planned journey aboard the *Jonathan* with details about the crew and provisions for the trip. A contract for what should happen, it's true, does not tell us what really occurred. But it was one more important piece of the New Hampshire founding puzzle.

Charles Deane is part of that puzzle. Every historian who writes about the past changes it. "No one knew better than Mr. Deane what the perils of investigation are, and how a tendency to jump at conclusions must be resisted," a Boston colleague wrote admiringly of him.

Born in Biddeford, Maine, in 1813, Deane attended an elite private school. But he was unable to attend college when the sudden death of his father forced him to support his family. Hired as a shopkeeper in Boston, he became fascinated in his spare hours reading about the original leaders of Virginia and New England. But the deeper Deane delved into old manuscripts, the more errors and guesswork he found in their interpretation. Nobody, it seemed, really cared about New Hampshire's first English fishers.

A savvy businessman, Deane was able to retire in 1848 and dedicate the next forty years of his life to scholarship and writing. Despite missing out on a college education, he immersed himself in private collections and public archives. He corresponded tirelessly with intellectuals and experts and amassed a library of 13,000 volumes. "No man loved his books more tenderly than Mr. Deane," a contemporary noted.

"The eye of history is TRUTH," Deane often said, quoting an early Greek writer. "I always like to see historical questions settled," he once told a room full of fellow antiquarians. Making order out of chaos, he knew, required huge chunks of time, frequent travel, significant expense, and much emotional investment.

"He dearly loved to drive the smallest error from the field," a historical society friend once wrote. "It was a pleasure for him to rehabilitate a forgotten fact." Recognizing his prolific work, both Harvard University and Bowdoin College eventually presented him with honorary degrees.

Deane's myth-busting was not always well received, as when he exploded the story that a lovesick young Indian princess Pocahontas had saved the life of Captain John Smith. Deane was surprised to find himself attacked by those who preferred the romantic Pocahontas legend to reality. Years later, when New Englanders became fascinated with tall, blond, blue-eyed Norsemen, Deane was skeptical of theories based on popular Viking sagas. "They are shadowy and mystical in form," he wrote, "and often uncertain in meaning."

Before Deane's discovery of the indenture, at least one

Massachusetts' writer had assigned Thompson to the scrapheap of history. Samuel Foster Haven, trained as a lawyer, served for almost half a century at the prestigious American Antiquarian Society in Worcester, Massachusetts. An expert in grants issued by the Council for New England, in 1869 Haven dismissed New Hampshire's first English settlers. "Whatever Thompson's grant may have been, it came to nothing," Haven wrote. The "supposed grant," Haven added, "if ever formally executed, was soon forfeited or abandoned" by Thompson and others.

Only 100 copies of Deane's essay on the 1622 indenture were published in 1876, intended for a small circle of the author's scholarly friends. The booklet included a crude reproduction of the flowery handwritten original, plus a full transcription of the indenture. In what is the most cogent essay ever written about David Thompson, Deane noted he was much more than a fisherman. David's name appears elsewhere in the records of the Council for New England as a sort of clerk, messenger, or emissary. He was, therefore, a person of note who would later, if only briefly, be considered the deputy governor of all New England.

Deane was an expert on the colonial era and his article should be taken seriously. He noted, for example, that the indenture specifically required Thompson to "build some houses for habitation" and to begin them "with as much expedition as may be." That instruction certainly distracts from the theory that Thompson had constructed Pannaway on a previous trip. Deane also made a strong case that the *Jonathan* probably left England early in January in order to catch the March fishing season.

Deane rejected the theory that the Hilton brothers established a second Piscataqua fishery in 1623. He also explained the confusion between Pannaway and the 1631 Great House or "Mason's Hall" at Strawberry Bank. And he tossed aside the false belief, still promoted today, that John Thompson, the son of David and Amias, was the first Englishman born in the colony of New Hampshire. In a single essay inspired by a single sheet of paper, Charles Deane blasted away a dozen misconceptions about the founding of New Hampshire.

Unfortunately, only a few nineteenth-century scholars were paying attention. Only those willing to dig deep could spot the footprints leading to the Thompsons' front door at Little Harbor. Collectively, the men who visited Pannaway in 1623 and soon after, offer us an origin story wholly unlike anything seen in a Thanksgiving Day pageant.

III. VISITORS

"There were also this year some scattering beginnings made in other places, as at Paskataway, by Mr. David Thomson [sic], at Monhegan, and some other places by sundry others."

— *William Bradford*, Of Plymouth Plantation, *written 1630-51*

"Another guest that winter night
Flashed back from lustrous eyes the light."

— *John Greenleaf Whittier*, Snow-Bound: A Winter Idyl, *1866*

"Exiled from the American origin story, Indigenous peoples await the telling of a history that includes them."

— *Ned Blackhawk*, The Rediscovery of America, *2023*

CHAPTER 12
Massacre at Wessagusset

By the autumn of 1621, half of the original *Mayflower* passengers were dead. Fifty-three survivors joined about ninety Wampanoag guests for a three-day harvest festival at New Plymouth. They ate deer, fowl, fish, eels, corn, and possibly lobster and wild turkeys. They did not use the word "thanksgiving," a term the Separatists reserved for a period of worship and devotion rather than feasting and games. So far, Edward Winslow wrote, the Natives under leader Massasoit had been "very trust[worthy], quick of apprehension, ripe witted, just." The multi-cultural event as reported by Winslow, however, was not the shape of things to come.

The Separatists, we should remember, were a Puritan group in that they wanted to purify the Church of England. Puritans wanted to remove what they considered the trappings of Catholicism that had crept into the official religion of England. This included certain prayers, incense, stained glass windows, the ornate vestments worn by priests, and the priests themselves. Anything that distracted worshippers from the Bible had to go. Most Puritans, including thousands who would soon flood into Massachusetts, believed it was possible to reform the Church of England. The Separatists (sometimes labeled as radical Puritans) did not. They insisted on total separation from what they considered a false religion. After years of isolation in Holland, a select few had come to build a religious utopia in a distant world.

The arrival of more colonists, most of them "strangers," not

Separatists, created a food crisis at New Plymouth. Meanwhile, it was rumored that nearby Natives who were enemies of Massasoit might exact revenge on Plymouth Colony. Fearing an attack, their paid military leader, Miles Standish, ordered the malnourished residents to "impale the town" inside a tall gated fence made of freshly cut logs, possibly pine or hemlock.

By the spring of 1622, after another grueling winter, the residents of New Plymouth were starving. There was an endless supply of cod, bluefish, and striped bass swimming just offshore, but according to modern historian Nathaniel Philbrick, "the Pilgrims were farmers, not fishermen . . . and they were unable to catch enough to feed themselves."

To the northeast, hundreds of European fishing vessels were at work off the coast of modern-day Maine and Canada. Desperate for food, Edward Winslow and a small Pilgrim crew sailed their shallop to Damariscove Island, now uninhabited off Boothbay Harbor. Damariscove was another project of Sir Ferdinando Gorges, who was no friend of the Pilgrims. Winslow found "about thirty sail of ships" there. Although typically described as a seasonal fishing outpost, experts have suggested it was an early year-round operation like Pannaway. The Damariscove fishers turned out to be friendly and generous to the Pilgrims.

The news coming from Jamestown that spring was devastating. A total of 347 colonists—men, women, and children—had been killed by Indians in Virginia. The death of a quarter of the English population there stoked fears among the Pilgrims that they might suffer a similar fate. Standish, in response, stepped up the training of his rag-tag militia and managed the construction of a crude fort at New Plymouth. Then, in midsummer 1622, a party of sixty "lusty men" led by Thomas Weston arrived from England aboard the ships *Swan* and *Fortune*.

Weston was the London agent who had negotiated a financial deal between the Separatists, then living in Holland, and the Merchant Adventurers who funded their *Mayflower* voyage. To date, the English investors had seen little, if any, return from the struggling Pilgrims. In the summer of 1622, Weston hoped to launch a profitable colony of his own. Known as Wessagusset, it was situated about twenty-two miles north of New Plymouth at what is today the town of Weymouth. Weston had shifted from a supporter of the Pilgrims to a competitor. Nineteenth-century historian Charles Francis Adams, Jr. called Wessagusset "ill-conceived, ill-executed, ill-fated."

Weston's fifty or sixty men spent July and August at New Plymouth, further stretching the colony's meager supplies. "They are so base in condition, for the most part," Governor Bradford later wrote of Weston's group, "as in all appearance not fit for honest men's company; and yet everything was done to make them comfortable." In September, they pushed into the heart of Indian territory to build their trading post. Within a year the fate of Wessagusset would shatter the brief peace on Cape Cod and send shockwaves to the first English settlers arriving in New Hampshire.

Frightened, cold, and hungry, buoyed only by their faith, the Pilgrims struggled simply to survive their third winter in New England. But things were much worse at Wessagusset, where Weston's settlers (he had returned alone to England) fell quickly into a state of despair. These were not adventurers, according to one Weymouth historian, but men "of the roughest material . . . picked up on the streets and on the docks of London." They had arrived too late in the season for planting and, lacking leadership, had consumed all their winter supplies. Taunted by the Natives, they hunkered close to their stockade, scrounging for clams, mussels, and groundnuts. Guards died of starvation at their post. A man who stole corn from the nearby Natives was executed by his fellow settlers.

Early in 1623, the Pokanocket great sachem Ousamequin (Massa-soit) warned Edward Winslow of a possible conspiracy. It was rumored that an alliance of Cape Cod tribes was planning to wipe out all the settlers at both Wessagusset and New Plymouth. The Pilgrims' only hope of survival, the sachem reportedly claimed, was to kill Wittawamut (also Wituwamat), a powerful war chief and leader of the plot. Although the danger was still only hearsay, in March, Pilgrim leaders agreed to send Standish, a Native guide named Hobomack, and seven men to mount a preemptive strike. Standish was instructed to return with the head of Wittawamut.

As the Pilgrim militia was about to sail, an exhausted settler named Phineas Pratt appeared outside the gates of New Plymouth. Formerly a London carpenter, Pratt had been among Weston's advance group assigned to find a suitable site for the new colony. In 1622, while searching for the best location, Pratt had been aboard a ship that visited Damariscove, the Isles of Shoals, and Cape Ann, before selecting Wessagusset.

But within months of their arrival at Wessagusset, Pratt explained to the Pilgrims, the unprepared colonists were facing starvation. Fleeing a desperate situation, Pratt had walked through deep snow without food, pursued by Indians "like a deer chased by the wolves," he later claimed. Pratt, too, believed local Natives were planning "to kill all English people in one day when the snow was gone."

One year after the Jamestown massacre, on March 23, 1623 (other accounts add a day or two), Standish and his men set out on a rescue and assassination mission. Whether Native leaders intended to follow through with their raid, or if there was a plan at all, we'll never know. Arriving by shallop, the Pilgrims discovered the Wessagusset outpost still intact. Standish invited chiefs Wittawamut and Pecksuit (or Pecksuot) and others to attend an impromptu peace negotiation in the blockhouse at Wessagusset. Pecksuit, according to contemporary accounts, told Standish that although he was a great captain, he was still a "little man." The tribal warriors agreed to sit down for a meal with the Pilgrim commander. In his bestselling book *Mayflower*, Nathaniel Philbrick describes what happened next:

> *Once they had all sat down and begun to eat, the captain signaled for the door to be shut. He turned to Pecksuot and grabbed the knife from the string around [his] neck. Before the Indian had a chance to respond, Standish had begun stabbing him with his own weapon. The point was needle sharp, and Pecksuot's chest was soon riddled with blood-spurting wounds. As Standish and Pecksuot struggled, the other Pilgrims assaulted Wituwamat and his companion.*

Seven Natives were slaughtered that day. Standish carried the head of Wittawamut back to New Plymouth, where his men were greeted as heroes. He mounted the severed head of the Indian warrior on a pole and displayed it on the roof of the fort.

According to Captain Emmanuel Altham, whom we met earlier, Governor Bradford sent Standish specifically "to bring away the head of him that made the broil." Altham appears to have arrived at New Plymouth after the 1623 massacre and remained there for months, so his account may be based on hearsay. Six months later, the severed head of the Pilgrims' "chief enemy" was still on public view. Instead of a flag, Altham wrote to his brother in England, "we have a piece of linen cloth dyed in the same Indian's blood which was hung out upon the fort when Massasoit was here."

Some Separatists struggled to justify Standish's action that violated their religious beliefs. Reverend John Robinson, the Separatist leader still living in exile in Holland, was displeased by the news. Fearing that his flock was turning to fanaticism, Robinson condemned the act in a letter to New Plymouth. Standish, Robinson said, should have converted the "poor Indians" to Christianity rather than murdering them without evidence of any crime. Reverend William Hubbard, the Puritan historian, claimed Standish had ignored Christ's first lesson—"to offer violence to no man." Later accounts often redacted the murders entirely, noting only that the brave Pilgrims "went to the rescue of their neighbors" at Wessagusset.

In his 1905 biography, *Captain Miles Standish*, Tudor Jenks described his subject as "quick-witted, bold, resourceful, and prudent." On the Wessagusset massacre, Jenks concluded, "It was a bloodthirsty proceeding, but necessary for the salvation of Plymouth. . . . One cannot see that they could have done otherwise."

American military historian Samuel Eliot Morison agreed. When a critic in the 1950s referred to Wessagusset as "Standish's treachery," Morison shot back. "A strange definition of treachery it seems to me!" Without the Pilgrim's preemptive strike, Morison argued, "they and all other English in New England would have been wiped out."

Weston's Wessagusset colony was abandoned. Most of the men returned to England or fled to fishing outposts in Maine. The indigenous population, meanwhile, was shattered. In his memoir, *Good News from New England*, published in 1624, Edward Winslow reported that Natives throughout the region "forsook their houses, running to and fro like men distracted, living in swamps and other desert places, and so brought manifold diseases amongst themselves, whereof very many are dead."

Already drastically reduced by European-borne diseases, Indians in hiding could not plant crops. Uncounted numbers died in the coming months of sickness and starvation. Tribes throughout the Cape Cod region avoided all contact with New Plymouth, thus crippling the English colony's ability to trade for Indian goods. This left the Pilgrims unable to repay their creditors back in England. The founders of New Plymouth who referred to themselves as "saints" were now known to the First People of New England as "wotawquenange" or "cutthroats."

John Kemp, Coordinator of Colonial Training at Plimoth

Plantation, pulled no punches on this topic. In his introduction to *Governor Bradford's Letter Book*, a collection of Pilgrim correspondence, Kemp wrote: "In fact, after all the lofty words about friendship and Christian love when the [New Plymouth] colony began, the colonists' lack of concern for their Pokanoket or Wampanoag neighbors just a few years later says a great deal about the nature of colonialism. Colonists don't like to think about the people they are colonizing."

CHAPTER 13
Pratt & Weston at Pannaway

As Miles Standish and his crew were murdering seven Native warriors at Wessagusset, David Thompson and his team were building Pannaway and hauling in their first bounty from the sea. The tragic and disturbing news from Plymouth Colony must have reached the fishermen at Little Harbor within days. According to Pilgrim journals, immediately following the massacre, a portion of the surviving Wessagusset men took their ship, the *Swan*, and sailed northeast to the fishing outposts on the Maine coast. Most of these starving and terrified men were finished with the New World. From these busy staging sites, they hoped to find passage back to England.

New Hampshire did not exist in 1623. (The name first appeared on a document in 1629.) There was only Thompson's fortified outpost at the mouth of the Piscataqua River. So the Isles of Shoals was the first stopping point for the men aboard the *Swan*. With the spring fish harvest in full swing, haggard Wessagusset survivors stopped at the Shoals to both recover their strength and recount their horrific adventure. Weston's men may have stayed on Smuttynose or at the adjacent rocky islands known today as Lunging, Star, Cedar, and Appledore.

We can't know who first visited Pannaway. If Thompson kept records, they have yet to be uncovered. We can, however, assemble a sketchy guest list from scraps of journals composed and published by his contemporaries. Phineas Pratt, the carpenter who warned the Pilgrims of trouble at Wessagusset, may have been the first fellow

Englishman to knock on Thompson's door. He later recalled what happened after the massacre. (This text has been modernized.)

> *At this time ships began to fish at the Islands of Shoals and I, having recovered a little of my health, went to my company near about this time. The first plantation at Piscataqua, the governor thereof, was Mr. David Thompson at the time of my arrival.*

If Pratt, as he claimed, had been among Thomas Weston's small scouting party that selected the site for Wessagusset Colony, then he had previously visited all the seasonal fishing sites along the coast. But Thompson's outpost was brand new. It was a sturdy year-round house set, not on an island, but on the mainland. It is only a fleeting mention, but Pratt called it "the first plantation" in the region.

Unlike his many companions, Phineas Pratt did not return to England, but settled at New Plymouth. He married Mary Priest, eighteen years his junior, who arrived from Leiden, Holland, aboard the *Anne* in July 1623. They had eight children and later moved to the budding village of Charlestown, Massachusetts.

David Thompson is mentioned in Pratt's memoir, *A Declaration of the Affairs of the English People*, that appeared in 1662. The account earned Pratt a grant for 300 acres of land from the General Court of Massachusetts Bay. His health failing, Pratt later applied for financial aid from the court in 1668 claiming to have been among the original settlers of the region. His request brought no relief and he died in 1680 at about ninety years old.

Almost two centuries after it was written, Phineas Pratt's detailed *Declaration* was discovered in the archives of the Massachusetts Statehouse. It is not an easy document to decipher and, critics point out, was composed three decades after the events of the 1620s. It was transcribed from three torn and sewn folio sheets and published in 1858.

A close reading appears to show Pratt encountered two Natives while he was staying at Pannaway. The Indians had traveled to Little

Harbor from their village near the abandoned outpost at Wessagusset. Their leader, a sachem known as Abbadakest (also Obtakiest) had survived the sudden attack by Miles Standish and his Pilgrim agents. In the fray, two of Weston's settlers were either captured or they elected to live among the Indians. Both English men were later executed in revenge for the Pilgrim attack.

According to Pratt, while he was staying at Pannaway the Natives taunted him. "When we killed your men they cried and made ill-favored faces," they said. Adapted into modern English, Pratt told the Indians, "When we killed your men, we did not torment them to make ourselves merry." Edward Winslow, curiously, attributes this brief encounter to Massasoit.

Phineas Pratt was not at the Wessagusset massacre, having made a harrowing winter escape pursued by Indians to New Plymouth. He was sheltering there when Standish returned bearing the severed head of Wittawamut swathed in a bloody cloth.

Scholars have accused Pratt of exaggerating his importance. He probably did. His claim for financial support was based on warning the Pilgrims of a possible Indian attack. The resulting massacre was not New Plymouth's finest hour. And besides, Pratt was one of "Weston's men," a less than stellar recommendation to a Puritan court.

If there is an arch villain in the *Mayflower* story, from a Separatist point of view, it is certainly Thomas Weston. After abandoning the Pilgrims in debt to the Merchant Adventurers of London, his poorly planned Wessagusset experiment might have led to the annihilation of New Plymouth. Weston is generally described as part trader and part explorer in the mold of Captain John Smith and Sir Walter Raleigh. He was a "freebooter," one Pilgrim historian wrote. "His head was full of schemes for deriving great and sudden gain from the settlement of the North American coast."

In the early summer of 1623, Weston also stumbled into Little

Harbor and begged David Thompson for help. Accompanied by a pair of fishermen from Monhegan Island, Weston was aboard a shallop en route to inspect what remained of his colony at Wessagusset. According to William Bradford, Weston's boat was wrecked in a storm somewhere between the Merrimack and Piscataqua Rivers and he almost died.

Reaching shore, Weston "fell into the hands of the Indians, who pillaged him of all he saved from the sea, and stripped him out of all his clothes." Wearing only his shirt, Weston managed to reach "Pascataquack" on foot. Thompson knew the ragged figure at his door. In July 1622, the Council for New England had assigned David Thompson to deliver a petition to the House of Lords. The petition informed the lords and the king of Weston's shady business deals in America.

Nevertheless, at Pannaway the Thompsons tended to Weston's wounds and gave him a fresh suit of clothes. Dressed and refreshed at Little Harbor, Weston brazenly returned to New Plymouth where, as we will see, he sparred with Governor Bradford and with Robert Gorges, the first governor of New England.

Historian Samuel Elliot Morison characterized Thomas Weston as "a small-time promoter . . . who chiseled in on the business of the great chartered companies of England." He likened Weston to a seventeenth-century loan shark, continually "milking the Pilgrims" with inflated expense accounts that kept them in debt to their investors for over two decades.

Weston's sleazy reputation is broadly portrayed in the 1952 Technicolor movie classic *Plymouth Adventure*. The film stars Spencer Tracy as a mean-spirited, sour-faced version of Christopher Jones, who captained the original *Mayflower*. Lloyd Bridges plays a bare-chested first mate who despises the strange religious fanatics. Thomas Weston, portrayed by Welsh character actor Rhys Williams, is a heartless, full-on bad guy. As the film opens, Weston bribes Captain Jones and his first mate to dump the Pilgrims off in New England, where they would hopefully starve or freeze to death. *Plymouth Adventure* is a cringe-worthy pseudo-history styled after a popular 1950s romance novel.

As the film ends, Captain Jones rejects Weston's evil plot. He comes to admire the Pilgrims and mercifully shelters them on the *Mayflower* for their first New England winter. Anchored aboard ship in Plymouth Harbor, William Bradford, played by actor Leo Genn, delivers a stirring pep-talk.

"What is the deadliest danger we now face?" Bradford declares before the Pilgrims go ashore. "Hunger, wild beasts, savages? No. The deadliest danger we face is that we may disagree—that we may each go grubbing in the wilderness for himself alone and so face quick destruction."

In 1625, David Thompson expressed a hauntingly similar sentiment in a letter mailed to the Council for New England. Thompson feared the American experiment might soon fail, due less from wild animals and Indians, but from lawless English fishermen, drunken English renegades, and reclusive English Separatists.

CHAPTER 14
Miles Standish, Fish-to-Go

Imagine the Thompsons' surprise, having heard of the grisly event at Wessagusset, to find the most dangerous man in New England standing at their door. Miles Standish, with his bushy red beard and fierce expression, is arguably the most recognizable figure to step off the *Mayflower*. Short in stature, he is often portrayed in a brimmed Morion-style metal helmet, gorget (throat armor), and breastplate. He also wore padded round breeches or "slops" and a padded jerkin over his linen shirt. He was equipped with an elegantly decorated rapier, a heavy matchlock musket, and a flowing cape.

The early life of the Pilgrim's one-man-army is little known. Standish was born around 1584. Whether he was a mercenary or served in the English army in the Low Countries (the Netherlands) is also a topic of debate. By 1620 he was living in Leyden, Holland, with his first wife, Rose. There he got to know the self-exiled Separatists from England before their 1620 journey into history.

Standish, for the record, was not the Pilgrims' first choice for military leader. Captain John Smith of Jamestown and Pocahontas fame had already visited, fished, mapped, and named New England. Smith's fee to serve as their military leader in Virginia (their original destination) may have been more than the Separatists could afford. Smith was rejected, he reported, because "my books and maps were much better cheap to teach them than myself."

Standish was parodied in the seventeenth century as the choleric "Captain Shrimp" and as a "little chimney [that] is quickly fired." Like other figures from New Plymouth, Standish was rediscovered and revered in the nineteenth century. New England historians, often Christian ministers, praised him as heroic, fearless, doughty, stalwart, and doggedly loyal to his Pilgrim employers. Whatever he did in the name of New Plymouth, Puritan historians implied, must have been righteous. Only months after his murderous encounter at Wessagusset, Standish was assigned to hunt for food.

Initially ineffective at fishing, the Pilgrims were forced to shop around. In 1622 Edward Winslow had sailed to Damariscove Island to barter for supplies from the fishermen there. By the following year, the food situation at New Plymouth was worse. Thompson's new outpost, barely half the distance to Damariscove, was worth a visit.

New Plymouth colonists, at first, were also failed farmers. Their optimistic system of communal property and collective farming quickly soured. Some felt exploited while others slacked off work. Discontent reigned until April, the month after the Indian massacre, when Pilgrim leaders agreed to portion out the land to every man, woman, and child, with each able to keep his or her harvest. This would quickly develop into a system of private property. The weather, however, did not cooperate, and by summer the corn was "parched like withered hay," William Bradford reported.

The fleet of seasonal fishermen at the Isles of Shoals had returned to England, their ships stocked with valuable dried and salted cod, and taking with them a few of the Wessagusset survivors. So as the Pilgrim corn dried on its stalks in the drought of 1623, Standish and his mini-militia found themselves at Pannaway. A deal was quickly struck. David Thompson loaded his own shallop with fish and followed Standish to New Plymouth.

Even as they arrived, the drought was broken by a gentle and refreshing rain that revived the dying crops. A single lengthy sentence in the Pilgrim record put Thompson on the map. It appeared in Winslow's *Good News from New England* published in London in 1624.

> *. . . At the same time Captain Standish being formerly employed by the Governor to buy provisions for the refreshing of the Colony, returned with the same, accompanied with one Mr. David Tomson [sic], a Scotchman, who also that Spring began a Plantation twenty-five leagues northeast from us, near Smiths Isles, at a place called Pascatoquack, where he liketh well. . .*

Winslow attributed the wounding dry spell as punishment from God. The healing rain and the delivery of Thompson's supplies, he reasoned, were sent from heaven, not humans. Winslow wrote:

> *So that, having these many signs of God's favor and acceptance, we thought it would be great ingratitude . . . [to] content ourselves with private thanksgiving for that which by private prayer could not be obtained. And so another Solemn Day was set aside and appointed for that end.*

Like many Puritan groups steeped in Calvinist tradition, the Pilgrims were always looking for signs that they were among their God's "elect" or chosen people. This sudden reversal of fortune in 1623, Winslow noted in his journal, was evidence of their divine favor. Their rescue by the Almighty, once more, from the brink of disaster required a dedicated period of fasting and prayer by the entire Pilgrim village. The theory that it takes the will of an entire congregation to speak to God is a bulwark belief of the Congregational Church that would soon spread throughout New England.

It is worth noting that Winslow assigned bad weather, not the murder of seven Natives, as the source of God's displeasure. During his visit, Thompson could not have missed the head of Wittawamut mounted on the roof of the fort that also served as a place of worship.

Two more ships arrived at New Plymouth that summer. The *Anne* and *Little James* brought around 100 new colonists who, whether saint or stranger, would each receive an acre of land. Phineas Pratt and the widowed William Bradford and Miles Standish would find wives among the new arrivals. Edward Winslow returned to England aboard the *Anne* in September with a supply of lumber and furs in order to report to the colony's investors. Winslow, the source of the Thanksgiving holiday story, would publish his book mentioning Thompson while in London the following year.

Winslow's reference to Thompson as a Scot has become so entangled in the historical record as to be unfixable. Again, although born in London, Thompson was raised by parents from Scotland. He probably spoke with a bit of a brogue. As previously noted, Winslow's use of the term "Scotchman" may have been freighted with darker meaning under the reign of King James I. It was King James, born in Scotland, and his persecution of the Separatists that they had traveled 3,000 miles to escape.

The Pilgrim leaders, therefore, had every reason to dislike and distrust David Thompson. He was undoubtedly a "Churchman" of the Anglican faith. Despite his status as an apothecary, he was currently managing a crew of fishermen, considered a lowly trade. Like the duplicitous Thomas Weston, the Pilgrim leaders considered him to be another "Gorges man." It was Thompson, one Pilgrim historian pointed out, "who had clothed the naked Weston" at Pannaway after the local Natives had robbed and stripped the London merchant.

Besides being a favorite of Sir Ferdinando Gorges, Thompson was tightly connected to the Council for New England. The Council, and especially Gorges, did not want to see New England dominated by what they considered a small cult of religious zealots.

The Pilgrims were also on edge in 1623 due to a visit by Francis West, who showed up in New Plymouth just a month before Thompson.

Representing the Council, West announced he was now "Admiral of New England." His mission, according to historian John Abbot Goodwin, was "driving from the coast all fishermen who had not taken a costly license with the Council." Many English fishermen resisted the new regulation. West quickly gave up his impossible assignment, but the strong-arm tactics of the Council reportedly reduced the English fishing fleet from 400 to 150 ships.

English shipowners, mostly from the West Devon coast, complained to Parliament that Sir Ferdinando Gorges and his group were trying to monopolize the New England fishing industry. They were. The renowned barrister and champion of individual freedom, Sir Edward Coke, not only challenged Gorges' authority to operate a monopoly, but questioned the monarch's right to issue exclusive patents to organizations like the Council. "Shall none visit the seacoast for fishing?" Coke proclaimed to Gorges in a hearing at Parliament. "If you alone are to pack and dry fish, you attempt a monopoly of the wind and sun!"

King James I, who claimed his divine right to rule came directly from God, simply ignored Coke's anti-monopoly legislation. But the rift between Parliament and the Crown was widening. In two years, James I would be dead from dysentery. His son and successor, King Charles I, would lose his head following the English Civil War and the rise of a Puritan leader named Oliver Cromwell.

In 1622, the year before Thompson's visit, the Pilgrims had found much-needed supplies during Winslow's emergency trip to Damariscove Island in Maine. The fishermen there had refused to accept payment. They were only doing "what they could freely," Winslow wrote joyfully, "wishing their store had been such as they might in greater measure have expressed their own love and supplied our necessities, for which they sorrowed." Thompson, however, certainly charged a reasonable fee for his long-distance delivery. The Pilgrim journal writers expressed no praise or even thanks for the man from Little Harbor. During a second encounter with Thompson in 1626, as we will learn, they were, again, without a kind word to say about him.

CHAPTER 15
Christopher Levett's Dream

Two more of Sir Ferdinando Gorges' empire builders found shelter at Pannaway in the fall of 1623. Robert Gorges, Ferdinando's son, had high hopes of reviving the failed settlement at Wessagusset. In the eyes of his father, the Council, and King James, Robert would be the first English governor of New England. How that played out, we'll soon see.

Christopher Levett, the other visitor to Little Harbor, was preparing to plant a colony of his own somewhere along the shores of northern New England. Born in York, England, the son of an innkeeper, Levett was a successful linen draper who longed to join the adventurous ranks of Sir Walter Raleigh, Sir Francis Drake, and Captain John Smith. A skilled mariner, Levett was also an expert in the science of harvesting tall straight trees that became the masts essential to English merchant and naval vessels. And he was a member of the Council for New England.

In the spring of 1623, as David Thompson's team salted and dried their latest catch in the Little Harbor sunshine, Levett was living with his second wife and six children in Somerset County, England. Then in May he got thrilling news. The Council had granted his patent for 6,000 acres in the "Province of Maine," the first time that phrase is known to appear in print. Levett promised to build a city he would call York, in honor of his birthplace. In his account titled *A Voyage to New England*, Levett opened with these words:

The first place I set my foot upon in New England was the Isles of Shoals, being islands in the sea about two leagues from the Maine. Upon these islands I neither could see one good timber nor such good ground as to make a garden.

Levett was less excited about the Shoals than his hero John Smith had been a decade earlier. There were no trees from which to build wooden flakes for drying fish. The islands were small and the harbor was "indifferent good," he wrote. Levett saw "no savages at all" on the nine barren islands. We now know indigenous people repeatedly visited the Shoals dating back at least 6,000 years. Levett's observation was recorded soon after the devastating Great Plague. His account continues:

The next place I came unto was Pannaway, where one Mr. Thompson hath made a plantation there. I stayed about one month in which time I sent for my men from the east who came over in diverse ships.

Although the weather was "unseasonable and very much snow," Levett explored the Piscataqua River during his stay with the Thompsons. He found plenty of good timber along the riverbank, but assumed the land was too rocky for farming. He did not—historians take note— encounter a settlement operated by the Hilton brothers at what would become Dover Point. Further upriver, a Native sagamore told him, the soil grew very fertile.

We should pause here to unpack a whispered local legend—that the Thompsons kept an enslaved Native in their household. The story, recounted in the mid-1800s by John Scribner Jenness, appears to have come from Phineas Pratt's 1662 petition to the Massachusetts Court.

Pratt briefly mentioned an incident when Captain Levett (he spelled the name "Louit") was staying at Pannaway. Translated into modern spelling, Pratt wrote: "A Sachem of Sagamore gave two of his men, one to Captain Levett & another to Mr. Thompson."

Someone in Pratt's narrative—it isn't clear who is speaking—then asks, "How can you trust these savages?"

Someone else responds, "Call the name of one Wat Tyler & the other Jack Straw, after the names of the two greatest rebels that ever were in England."

The reference is to the Peasants' Revolt of 1381, obscure today, but well known in the seventeenth century. Also known as Tyler's Rebellion, the incident involved a medieval march on London by disgruntled English "commoners." The riot resulted in concessions by King Richard II. Wat Tyler was killed in the fray and Jack Straw ended up as a character in Chaucer's *Canterbury Tales*.

A number of powerful figures, including the Archbishop of Canterbury, were murdered during the uprising as a mob stormed the Tower of London. The speaker in Pratt's narrative appears to be warning Thompson against bringing an Abenaki Native inside the walls of Pannaway. Whether Thompson accepted the "gift" of an indigenous servant, whether enslaved, indentured, or employed, is unknown.

Striking out with his crew in two small open boats, Levett explored the Maine region along the Agamenticus waterway (York River). He visited Cape Porpoise, Saco, and Biddeford Pool (where Richard Vines had settled years earlier). Trapped in a blizzard for five days, sleeping on the frozen ground, Levett cheered his men with witty anecdotes and Bible stories. By all accounts, his contacts with the Natives he encountered were extremely cordial.

But it was the site of the future city of Portland that ticked all the right boxes. The design of the harbor, its islands, and the abundance of timber, fish, and fowl convinced Christopher Levett to claim his 6,000 acres there. He proudly named the future colony "York" in honor of his birthplace. It was, one nineteenth-century pundit quipped, the first "New York" in the New World.

Leaving ten fishermen working at a freshly fortified outpost at

Casco Bay, Levett caught a trading ship home, probably during the summer of 1624. Back in England he began soliciting investors to bankroll his planned settlement. Wealthy, well-educated, and well-connected, Levett was ideally suited to launch a profitable English colony.

By establishing permanent coastal towns, he argued, merchants could cash in on both spring and fall fishing seasons, doubling their income. More settlements, he reasoned, meant more fish. More fish meant more shipbuilding. More ships meant more poor people could emigrate to the colonies, thus releasing the population burden on English villages and cities. England, Levett argued, should immediately secure her fishing settlements against the encroaching French and harvest the abundant timber and fur resources in New England.

Even James I openly favored Levett's plan to build the Anglican city of York in the wilderness of Maine. Best remembered for commissioning a popular translation of the Bible that bears his name, King James suggested that Levett's funding should come from churches. To attract church funding, Levett promised to propagate the king's official religion among the Natives by "converting those ignorant people to Christianity."

Within twenty years, Levett promised, there would be no more poverty in England and a thriving colony across the sea. It was an intriguing thesis. Then King James died. And as is so often the case, the chaotic politics of England that followed shaped the history of New England a world away.

In March 1625, as Levett continued his search for investors, Charles I ascended to the British throne. Within two months, the Anglican king was married by proxy to fifteen-year-old Henrietta Maria, a Roman Catholic princess from France. Christopher Levett was drawn into the new king's service as the captain of a warship in a failed expedition against the Spanish.

Levett's alliance to George Villiers, the Duke of Buckingham, did not improve his reputation. A flamboyant court favorite of both James I and Charles I, Buckingham was unpopular with the public and even less popular with a Parliament that was increasingly at odds with its new king. In a twist of fate, Buckingham was later assassinated in Portsmouth, England, while lodging at the home of Captain John Mason. Two years later, in 1630, Mason would launch a New Hampshire colony known as Strawberry Bank.

It was during this chaotic period, with his colonial hopes fading, that Christopher Levett published his brief *Voyage to New England* (1629). While Levett makes only a cameo appearance in Granite State history, he is well remembered in Maine. His 1623-24 survey of the coastal frontier is richly detailed and engagingly candid. Although, like his contemporaries, Levett referred to the Natives he met as "savages," his account demonstrates true respect and affection for these kindly, friendly, resourceful, and sophisticated people.

No one was more curious about Levett than nineteenth-century Portland mayor, James Phinney Baxter. As president of the Maine Historical Society for three decades, Baxter's research on Levett took him deep into archives while traveling in England. In 1897, Baxter produced a brief biography of Portland's first European settler. If not for Levett's ability to "wield a ready pen," Baxter admitted, "his very name would have been buried in oblivion." If not for Baxter, that would be doubly true.

Levett devoted much of his narrative in *Voyage* to a study of indigenous culture, language, and religion. Much in the same way he might have analyzed the harvesting of timber, Levett described Native marriage practices, parenting, weaponry, clothing, cooking, and more. "Their houses are built in half an hour's space," he noted, "being a few poles or boughs stuck in the ground and covered with the bark of trees." He conversed with a sagamore about the Native concepts of good and evil. Upon learning the English monarch had only one wife, the Native leader laughed. King Charles, the sagamore said, must not be very powerful.

Unlike the marketing hype about New England published by others, Levett promised readers he would not "speak more than is true." The country delivered frigid weather and deep snow in winter, he admitted, and ravenous insects in the spring. Corn did not grow naturally on trees. "Nor will the deer come when they are called," Levett wrote, "nor stand still and look on a man until he shoot him. . . nor the fish leap into the kettle. . . or are they so plentiful you may dip them up in baskets."

Yet, in Baxter's words, Levett promised his investors "a country capable of being made more profitable than the West Indies, for her fisheries alone were richer than the mines of other countries."

While confessing he never sailed further south than the Isles of Shoals, Levett questioned whether settling at Massachusetts—inhabited by Separatists—might be overrated. At least four of the ten men Levett left at Casco Bay were refugees of the Wessagusset Massacre, which may have colored his view of Pilgrim justice. Those ten men, for the record, were never seen or heard from again.

Captain Christopher Levett's dream did not come true. Unable to raise the necessary funds to recreate the city of York, he never returned to Maine. Levett showed up momentarily in Salem, Massachusetts in 1630, but on his return to England that same year, he died aboard ship and was buried at sea.

CHAPTER 16
Robert Gorges, Reluctant Governor

Despite having failed again and again since 1607 to sustain a permanent Anglican colony in New England, Sir Ferdinando Gorges and his Council refused to give up. With the Thompson and Levett and other projects under development in 1623, Sir Ferdinando sent his son, Robert, to plant another trading and fishing post. The group intended to revive the abandoned site of Wessagusset, later the town of Weymouth on Boston Bay.

When Captain Christopher Levett arrived at Pannaway in the fall of 1623, Robert Gorges was waiting for him at Thompson's rough-hewn outpost. In a moment that might have ranked with the signing of the Mayflower Compact in 1620, the first English governing body was formed in what would become New Hampshire. Our only eyewitness account of the ceremony at Pannaway comes from Levett's memoir.

"At this place I met with the Governor who came thither in a bark which he had from one Mr. Weston about 20 days before I arrived in the land," Levett wrote.

It's a confusing detail. Why was Robert Gorges in Thomas Weston's boat? But Levett's reference checks out. Following the failure of his colony at Wessagusset, Weston had been engaged in fishing without obtaining a license from the Council for New England. The Council, especially Sir Ferdinando, considered this an illegal operation and put Weston on their most-wanted list.

Having survived his recent pillaging by the Indians and having been given a fresh suit of clothes by Thompson at Pannaway, Thomas Weston was recovering his health at New Plymouth when Robert Gorges arrived there from England with a boatload of new settlers. Francis West, whom we met earlier, was also at New Plymouth. As "Admiral of the Country," West was the Council's new one-man ocean-going police force.

Beyond the burden of planting a colony, Robert Gorges was the newly appointed "Lieutenant-General over all New England." He had brought 120 colonists aboard the ships *Katherine* and *Prophet Daniel*. They were "of a much higher grade" than Weston's "lusty men," according to Pilgrim leaders. Many of these men were accompanied by their wives and children. Besides mechanics and farmers, the newcomers included two Anglican ministers who were to act as spiritual leaders for New England, a potentially threatening issue for the Pilgrims.

Governor Gorges and Admiral West were on an impossible mission. They were assigned to capture anyone fishing along the New England coast without a license from the Council 3,000 miles away. As Puritan William Hubbard reported in his 1680 history, their job was "preventing and reforming all such evils and abuses as had been complained of to be committed by the fishermen and others." But countless hundreds of fishermen were, by now, part of the lucrative seasonal trade. Worse yet, according to Hubbard, some "lewd and wicked men" were committing atrocities among the Natives, bringing reproach upon the king and the English nation. Beyond policing the sea, Gorges and West were required to stop any man openly abusing Native women or "teaching their people drunkenness, with other beastly demeanors."

"Besides these remarkable powers," according to nineteenth-century historian James Phinney Baxter, "the Council could control the entire commerce of New England." The Council, Baxter explained, was theoretically in charge of every ship at every New England port. Their agents had the right to imprison and punish any captain or crewman under the often brutal laws of England. Missing, however, was the Council's ability to enforce its wide-ranging authority. Captain Robert Gorges, a little known figure, was only twenty-seven in 1623. We have no evidence that he had a wife or family and, other than having served in the British Navy, Robert's early days are cloaked in mystery.

Colliding with Thomas Weston was Robert Gorges' first big test as governor. The most powerful Englishman in New England—on paper at least—Robert summoned Weston to account for his crimes. The showdown at New Plymouth, according to William Bradford, was no contest. When Gorges accused Weston of sowing the seeds for the tragedy at Wessagusset, Weston said he wasn't there. The fault was with his men. Robert then cited Weston for illegally selling off the cannons he had obtained for his settlement to Turkish pirates, leaving Sir Ferdinando holding the bill. At first, Weston said nothing. Then he began insulting the young governor and mocking his authority. Rising in defense, according to Bradford's journal, Robert Gorges flew into a rage and "vowed that he would either curb [arrest] him, or send him home to England."

At this point, if we can trust our Pilgrim narrator, Thomas Weston realized he might actually end up in chains. He grew contrite and begged Bradford to intercede on his behalf. Mollified by Bradford's defense and preferring peace over conflict, Robert Gorges let Weston go free on his own word. But as soon as the young governor's back was turned, Bradford added, Weston began mocking Sir Ferdinando's gullible son.

With his new crop of colonists at work rebuilding the Wessagusset settlement, Robert Gorges seized Weston's shallop and sailed to Little Harbor. Christopher Levett picked up the story from here:

> *The Governor then told me that I was joined with him in commission as a councilor, which being read, I found it was so. And he then, in the presence of three more of the Council, administered unto me an oath.*

It appears that Admiral Francis West was also sworn in at Pannaway, as was David Thompson, who would serve as "deputy" to Governor Robert Gorges. Henry Burrage, a Baptist minister and early president of the Maine Historical Society, recognized this as an historic moment. "The government of New England was now effected," Burrage wrote at the tercentenary of the event in 1923. Here in one room were the duly appointed representatives of the king. Governor Robert Gorges held the authority to enact laws and establish courts at his pleasure, both on land and at sea. Had things gone as planned, this New Hampshire meeting might have reshaped American history.

But Robert was not the hammer his father hoped to forge. He had let Weston go free instead of bringing him to justice. And like Weston, Robert let his own settlers down. Having arrived too late in the season for planting and meeting bad weather, Robert's people were forced to shelter for the winter inside the crude Wessagusset stockade. This was not what the future pioneers of New England had signed up for. Instead of beauty and bounty, wrote historian Charles Francis Adams Jr., they were "locked up in a desert of ice and snow—locked up in a log hut on the edge of a salt marsh with a howling unexplored forest behind and round about them."

Bad news arrived that winter in a letter from Sir Ferdinando. Public and political opinion against monopolies was on the rise. The Council for New England was bleeding members or, as Robert's father colorfully put it, they were "a carcass in a manner breathless." Money was tight. No more supply ships were coming for Robert's colonists. It was time, Sir Ferdinando suggested, for his son to come home "till better occasion should offer itself unto him."

By spring 1624, Robert Gorges' settlers had largely disbursed. Some fled to Virginia aboard the *Katherine*. Others, including Governor Gorges, went home to England on the *Prophet Gabriel*. A few, assisted by the Pilgrims, managed to survive at what would become the village of Weymouth in the Massachusetts Bay Colony.

Bradford could not have been happier to see the back of the reluctant governor. Robert Gorges, he wrote, "scarcely saluted the country. . . not finding the state of things here to answer his quality and condition."

History has not been kind to Robert Gorges. He died of an unknown illness at twenty-eight, soon after his return to England in 1624. Charles Francis Adams, Jr. minced no words in his history of early Massachusetts. Adams, the son and grandson of two American presidents, described Thomas Weston and Governor Gorges as "men of the most ordinary type—the one by nature a coarse English huckster, the other an ambitious and apparently brainless boy."

Historian Hubbard, who was among the first nine graduates of Harvard College in 1642, took a more philosophical view:

> By this experience of Captain Robert Gorges, it appears how great
> a difference between the theoretical and practical of an enterprise.
> The utopian fancy of any projector may, early in imagination, frame
> a flourishing plantation in such a country as New England, but to
> the actual accomplishing, thereof, there is required a good number
> of resolved people qualified with industry, experience, prudence, and
> estate, to carry on such a design to perfection, much of which were
> wanting in the present design.

Critics agree. The Separatists were driven by desperation and bound by a shared religious fervor. They were never going home. Merchant adventurers like Robert Gorges, by contrast, were not committed to America heart-and-soul. This time, Reverend William Hubbard's commentary was on the mark. Had he been around to advise Sir Ferdinando, Hubbard might have said—Be careful what you wish for and don't send a boy to do a man's work.

IV. MOVING ON

"[The Pilgrims] soon discovered where they should have settled. As they sailed their shallop across the island-speckled immensity of modern Boston Harbor, they were filled with envy."
— Nathaniel Philbrick in Mayflower, 2006

"Who thinks of the forgotten dead, once as active and useful inhabitants of this town as yourselves?. . . These streets will be trodden by men who will think no more of us than we do of the first settlers of the town."
— Reverend Edwin Holt from a sermon at North Church, Portsmouth, NH, 1838

"Still, the Plymouth Colony, by itself, wrought no nobler or better work for mankind than the unnoticed, almost unnamed colonists who founded New Hampshire."
— Nineteenth-century Dartmouth professor Edwin Sanborn in Granite Monthly

CHAPTER 17
David's Amazing Letter Home

Across the seas of time, like a message in a bottle, an all but forgotten note from David Thompson survives. In July 1625, he penned a three-page letter to Thomas Howard, the 14th Earl of Arundel. Howard was among three dozen members of the Council for New England, the joint stock company chartered to set up colonies in North America. An influential politician and diplomat under monarchs James I and Charles I, Howard traveled widely. He became an avid, if not obsessive, collector of sculptures, prints, books, drawings, and jewelry. At his death, the collection exceeded 700 pieces. His "Arundel marbles" included dozens of statues and over 100 marble busts. Excavated in Greece in the early 1600s, they are now housed at the Ashmolean Museum in Oxford, England.

We get our only true peek inside Thompson's brain thanks to Mary H.S. Hervey, an English art historian. Hervey spent a decade researching Thomas Howard. A transcript of David's letter was buried deep in the appendix of Hervey's book, *The Life, Correspondence, and Collections of Thomas Howard, Earl of Arundel*, published in 1921.

Most studies of Howard and his wife, Countess Aletheia, focus on them as patrons of the arts. Their famed collection included works by Titian, Tintoretto, da Vinci, Rubens, Van Dyck, Holbein, Correggio, Durer, and Raphael.

Relegated to the Arundel family archives for centuries, David Thompson's plaintive report to the Earl seems to have slipped between the cracks in the founding story of the Granite State. And yet, it is enormously significant to our understanding of the man and his times. It deserves the attention of future scholars. (We might even call it "The Missing Ink.") The transcription in Mary Hervey's book follows the spelling of Thompson's original hand-written letter, but even that is daunting to modern readers. So rather than reproduce the letter, for our purposes, we will hit the highlights.

Fully aware that the Earl was a collector of sculptures and jewelry, David Thompson began his report from America by mentioning what he believed to be chunks of gray marble discovered while he was at Naumkeag (Salem). He also saw a Native with a tobacco pipe he believed might be made of alabaster. Then, setting his friendly greeting aside, David got down to business.

"No man need expect any better place than the Massachusetts," he told Arundel. Nowhere to the north or south could compare. There were enough deer, fish, fowl, and good soil to accommodate 10,000 people, David suggested. Five years later, with the Great Migration, his prediction came true.

The primary threat to the future colonization of New England, he continued, were the "renegades" with their "excessive drunkenness" and "other vices I dare not name." This may be a reference to Thomas Weston's "lusty men" at Wessagusset. David also knew Thomas Morton and his maypole crowd at Mare Mount, who we will explore in detail soon. These profiteers, David told Arundel, were spoiling the Indian fur trade. What could be bought from the Natives for a thousand beads only two years earlier, had inflated to 6,000 beads.

Morton would be kicked out of Massachusetts twice for selling and bartering guns to the local tribes. According to Thompson, British traders were providing guns with barrels from four to six feet long. Indians were also buying European pistols, swords, powder, and shot.

"I have taken pieces from some of them [Natives], and told them his Majesty wills them to use their bows and not our pieces. They are grown so expert as that they exceed most of the English."

"We daily discover in the country greater and greater multitudes of savages," he continued. "Also, they are beginning to grow very arrogant and insult over some."

Two years after landing in New England, David Thompson was frightened. Despite his reputation for cooperating with indigenous people, he felt mounting danger. And the danger was coming, not from pirates, wolves, or Indians, but from the English.

His letter to the Earl of Arundel was posted from "Plymesland in New England." Of the Pilgrims—he called them "Brownists" after Separatist leader Robert Browne—Thompson had nothing positive to say. "They desire the society of none but such as are of their own profession, so I am assured none regards them or their fellowship," he told Thomas Howard.

Unlike the factional, even cultist Separatists, most New England settlers sent by the Council to date, had been independent adventurers like himself. Most were Anglicans, loyal to the Crown. They were not seeking religious freedom, but hoped to carve a profitable living out of America. In an effort to populate the region, David warned, the Council had spread its plantations too far apart.

"We are dispersed 16 leagues, 15 leagues, 12 leagues, 7 leagues and 2 leagues asunder," David reported. "And so none of us is able, therefore, to advertise one another or succor one another if need should require."

Halfway into his urgent letter, David drove his primary message home. "We are like a body without a head, none to rule us, none to minister justice, [settle] grievances among us, none to redress, especially among the Brownists of New Plymouth." Without necessities like clothes, powder, and shot, and with no means to import more cattle and more people, they were "like to be overthrown," he wrote.

These are not the words of some illiterate fishmonger or a lackey of Ferdinando Gorges. Having been little more than a cardboard character in local history, it is within this single letter that David Thompson comes alive. His skill as a businessman, a negotiator, a politician, a journalist, even as a potential leader, is evident on the page. He saw things as they were and skillfully delivered his message to one of the most powerful men in England.

"I have often called to mind the speeches used in your honorable chamber, speaking of the South Colony," he continued, referencing Jamestown. "A sword put in a madman's hand, a child's hand, or a fool's hand is dangerous. What can be expected that a rude, ignorant mechanic can do with a sharp sword of justice?"

David Thompson did not live in an age that embraced democracy or equality. People in seventeenth-century England were born servants or kings, rich or poor, bad or good. In 1625, he feared, New England was at a tipping point. There were too many reclusive Separatists, lawless fishermen, armed Indians, and drunken renegades. Please tell the king, "for Gad's sake," David begged his patron, to balance the scales by sending "some good people" and a leader to govern them. If not, their American investment was facing "utter destruction and overthrow."

"May we know his Majesty's pleasure of the continuance of us here," he asked in closing, "which is impossible without more people?" Beyond the legal obligations stated in his indenture, he was also a husband and a father who had put his family at risk. Can we come home now?—he begged, between the lines.

But David's timing was all wrong. Three months earlier, on March 27, 1625, James I had died at age fifty-eight following a stroke at his hunting lodge. The monarch was buried a month later under the altar at Westminster Abbey. It is unclear from David's letter whether the news had reached him. The ascension of James' son, Charles I, was a rocky time for the Earl of Arundel. He was intimately involved with the unpopular marriage between King Charles and his Catholic princess, Henrietta Maria, from France. Arundel was also part of the new king's coronation. But following a social scandal, he fell out of favor with Charles I and was briefly imprisoned in the Tower of London.

Did the Earl of Arundel write back? We don't know. The Council for New England, meanwhile, was on hiatus. Military men like Sir Ferdinando Gorges, John Mason, and Christopher Levett were called into service. Maritime raids against France and Spain during this period did not go well. By the time the joint stock group was up and running again, David Thompson was no more.

CHAPTER 18
An Island in Boston

Without further evidence, it is impossible to pin down exactly when David Thompson left New Hampshire. But from mid-1623, with the Council for New England temporarily out of business, he was effectively on his own. David's letter to the Earl of Arundel makes his motivation clear. Little Harbor was too far from the action. His outpost was too small to defend or maintain. David knew he had to move. And he knew, from his travels, where the heart of New England was about to begin beating.

Stepping boldly beyond his social status, after a humbling apology, David offered Arundel and the Council for New England a stirring piece of advice in his only letter home. "In my opinion," he wrote in July 1625, "it were most necessary that all the land plantations in the country should be forced to draw together to live in the Massachusetts."

Furthermore, David urged, all future English plantations should be required to include no fewer than forty, fifty, or sixty individuals. It was essential "that they might have one general governor" to run things. This letter, we should note, was written the year after Governor Robert Gorges had fled the scene. David implied that future leaders should be made of sterner stuff, which may be why he wrote to Arundel, rather than to Sir Ferdinando, Robert's father.

The more we analyze his decision, the more sense it makes. Having left a safe and spacious apartment in England, David, Amias, and young John were then living in the hinterland. Their fortress was mounted with guns and wrapped in a protective wooden palisade. Beyond a few fishermen and the occasional visiting dignitary, they were the only Europeans alive for a hundred miles. During the peak fishing seasons in spring and fall, the Isles of Shoals might be mobbed with hard-working hard-drinking fishermen. But in the months between they were isolated.

And judging from his letter to Arundel, David was not getting along with men of the Atlantic fishing trade. They were, he wrote, the most careless of all the people sent to New England. These fishermen were the most likely to quarrel with the Indians and to steal their kettles, animal skins, and more "as this year they have done," he wrote. His warning brings new meaning to Portsmouth's celebratory claim that its founders merely "came to fish."

The self-centered Brownists at New Plymouth, according to David, were not fit to run the region. Robert Gorges was back in England and, by this time, probably dead. Admiral Francis West, appointed by the Council to police the fishermen, had moved to Virginia. Captain Christopher Levett was campaigning, unsuccessfully, to fund his colonial city of York. Of the men who had sworn an oath at Pannaway to protect and govern New England, David Thompson was the last man standing. And here in his letter home, he made an extraordinary suggestion—one that rarely, if ever, has appeared in histories of New Hampshire. He begged the king and Council to send some "discreet" man to oversee the struggling plantations of New England.

> Captain John Mason in Foster Lane, formerly governor of a
> plantation in Newfoundland and now, as I understand, in England,
> were a fit instrument to this effort.

Five years before Mason organized a settlement at Strawberry Bank, Thompson predicted the man who would take his place as the founder of New Hampshire. In 1625, he asked Mason through his letter to the Earl of Arundel, to rescue everything the Council had created and immediately take his place as acting governor of New England. "Whoever shall undergo such a charge," he added, "should be experienced herein." To send more unskilled governors would be the ruin of the region, he argued. Robert Gorges, the Pilgrim leaders, and Francis West were not fit for the job, David implied, nor was he.

The troublesome Thomas Weston was also gone, but his attempt to start a colony had revealed a critical truth. While the Pilgrims had groped their way to a satisfactory building site at New Plymouth in 1620, it wasn't ideal. Boston Bay was better. Miles Standish had seen its advantages during his early exploration in 1621. In a more careful search in 1622, Weston's scouting party, including Phineas Pratt, had chosen Wessagusset, a spot barely thirty miles north of New Plymouth.

David Thompson had seen the future up close. He was on the scene when Robert Gorges tried to rebuild the failed Wessagusset site. It is beyond coincidence that David picked his second outpost nearby. In *A Documentary History of Chelsea* (1908), Mellen Chamberlain suggested Thompson was hired by the Council to help Robert Gorges restart Wessagusset. When, following his father's advice, Robert abandoned his colonists in 1624, David may have assisted those settlers who stayed to establish nearby Winnisimmet, a more defensible site with a better harbor and more fertile farmland. It is here that Samuel Maverick built his "palisade house," reportedly with David Thompson's help.

So instead of life on the Piscataqua, David chose a 170-acre island in Boston Bay with rolling hills and salt marshes. Still unspoiled and privately owned, it sits barely a mile from the mainland near Dorchester, Wollaston, and Jamaica Plain. Moving to Thompson Island, as it is still known, would place his fishing and trading operation just a short hop from modern day Weymouth and an afternoon's sail to his customers at New Plymouth.

Ironically, among the first white men known to have visited Thompson Island was Miles Standish. That detail comes from an early case argued before the Massachusetts General Court. In 1648, John Thompson, David's grown son, petitioned the court for ownership of his father's island. By the time of John's appeal, the island was considered part of the growing town of Dorchester. Standish, then in his mid-sixties, told the court he had landed there while exploring the future Boston Harbor aboard his shallop in September 1621. Standish reportedly named it "Island Trevore" (also Trevoyre or Trevour) after his shipmate, William Trevore. In his deposition, Standish added that David Thompson had shown him a patent including the term "Isle Thompson," then Standish hesitated. "But the terms of it I cannot remember," he told the court. Was the reference to Great Island at Little Harbor? Was Boston always Thompson's final destination? Standish's comment could launch a fleet of scholarly articles.

Adding to the confusion, William Trevore later testified he had taken possession of the island in 1619. Trevore claimed he had told David Thompson about his island while in London, and that Thompson had then secured his own patent for it. New England storyteller Edward Rowe Snow, advancing that theory, wrote that when in London, "Thompson had asked Trevore to pick out a likely island for him." The facts don't seem to agree. William Trevore may not have been in the country until he arrived aboard the *Mayflower* in 1620.

Another witness told the Massachusetts Court that Thompson had agreed to let others keep their hogs on his island. A Native identified as the "Sagamore of Agawam" testified that in 1619 "or thereabouts," he went with David Thompson who took possession of the island. Could the Sagamore have met Thompson at a later date? Or did Thompson visit the region earlier, as some have claimed? Did the meeting happen at all? There are too few pieces from which to view the puzzle.

Robert Earle Moody, a history professor at Boston University, suggested that David Thompson probably hoped to swap his promised Piscataqua land grant for the preferred island in Massachusetts. That exchange was codified when the court granted John Thompson his father's island, but with a caveat. In accepting Thompson Island, John had to give up all claims to any other land title, promise, or gift offered to his family by the Council for New England. According to John's testimony, his father occupied and built a habitation in Boston Bay about 1626. John would have been seven at the time. Samuel Maverick, who became John's stepfather after David's death, confirmed the date.

Like Christopher Levett at the Isles of Shoals, Standish saw no Indians during his visit to what would become Thompson Island. This was, of course, following the plague brought by European fishermen that left up to ninety percent of Natives dead. In the nineteenth century, when the island housed a farm school for boys, its former history as a popular indigenous occupation was obvious to all.

A 1910 article in the Boston Farm and Trades School newspaper reads: "One proof that our Island was inhabited by Indians is the relics hewn out of stone which are occasionally found. The kinds of relics are arrow-heads, spear-heads, corn pounders or pestles, war clubs, tomahawks, and sometimes gun flint." Archaeological research has since confirmed artifacts unearthed on Thompson Island date to the Late Archaic era (6,000 to 3,700 years ago). We know from many other digs that indigenous people thrived in New England for at least 12,000 years before Standish, Thompson, and Trevore were born.

Reverend Jeremy Belknap, who published the first history of New Hampshire in 1784, added to the confusion. Relying on William Hubbard's flawed coverage, Belknap claimed Thompson, "not being pleased with his situation, removed the next spring to an island in Massachusetts." Despite efforts by later editors to correct Belknap's often-quoted text, writers have passed on the false perception that

Thompson left Little Harbor in 1624. Drawing from Belknap and Hubbard, in 1809 the Massachusetts Historical Society reported Thompson "took possession" of this island six years before Boston was settled in 1630. What goes around, comes around.

Taking possession of the island was one thing, but moving there was quite another. Yet even Nathaniel Adams, author of the first history of Portsmouth (1825), bought into Hubbard and Belknap's error. Adams concluded Thompson spent only a year in New Hampshire. All three historians, it turns out, were wrong by at least two years. It may seem incidental, but this misconception helps explain why the Thompsons have received so little attention when, in fact, their move to Boston Bay speaks volumes about a critical moment in the founding of New England.

According to Hubbard, David Thompson left the Piscataqua "out of dislike either to the place or his employers." Thompson's second New England home, Hubbard wrote, was "a very fruitful island and desirable neck of land." That neck of land called "Squantum" became a neighborhood of Dorchester and later Quincy, Massachusetts.

New Hampshire's founding family spent at least three years at Pannaway. Arriving at Boston Bay late in 1626 or early 1627, Amias Thompson could finally mingle with the Anglican community of English settlers who occupied Wessagusset and Winnisimmet. Boston Bay offered her social, political, and financial benefits she could not find at Little Harbor. Amias finally had room to expand, graze animals, farm the fertile soil, add acres of fish-drying flakes, and attend to her son John. Things were looking up. But for David—the end was near.

CHAPTER 19
David Disappears

We have unshakable proof that David Thompson was still in charge at Little Harbor in 1626. Our farewell view of him comes from William Bradford, the now famous Pilgrim governor of New Plymouth. The evidence appears in Bradford's famous journal, *Of Plymouth Plantation,* completed in 1651, but not published until 1856. The 270-page vellum-covered manuscript, by the way, disappeared from the tower of Boston's Old South Meeting House during the American Revolution. It reappeared in England, was returned to the United States in 1897, was republished in 1912, and rests today at the Massachusetts State House in Boston.

The Pilgrims were still heavily in debt to their sponsors back in England. They had never been effective at commercial fishing and had all but run out of goods to trade with the Indians for furs. In 1626, they learned that a fishing operation at Monhegan Island was breaking up and selling off its goods. William Bradford, his fellow Separatist leader Edward Winslow, and a small crew quickly set sail from New Plymouth heading to Maine in a small open boat. According to Bradford, they stopped at Little Harbor on their way. Learning of this rare opportunity, David Thompson asked to go along.

For the next couple of days, Thompson kept company with the two men whose extensive journals have shaped American history. As the shallop cut through the waves along the coast of Maine, Thompson had an idea. Rather than bid against each other as rivals and drive up the price of goods, why not buy everything together, then split the cost down the middle? The Pilgrims agreed. The group bought whatever was available, including a few goats and some Biscay rugs the fishermen had salvaged from a French ship wrecked off the Maine coast. The total bill came to 500 pounds each, which they bartered for beaver pelts and corn.

"Mr. Thompson," Bradford pointed out, "having somewhat exceeded his resources, asked them to relieve him of some of his purchase." The merchant, who happened to be from Bristol, England, agreed to let them take the goods and pay the balance in a year. The bargain hunting expedition, it turns out, allowed the Pilgrims to renew trade with the Natives and get enough pelts to pay off some of the debt to their English sponsors.

About 250 years later, historian John A. Goodwin mentioned Thompson in *The Pilgrim Republic* (1879). According to Goodwin, "the voracious Thompson. . . a shrewd Scotchman," managed to swindle Bradford and Winslow into paying more than their fair share, an interpretation not found in Bradford's original text. Goodwin, for the record, has been described as a "beloved disciple" of the Pilgrims. He dedicated his book to Standish, Winslow, and Bradford—"the wise, the brave, the able Triumvirs." The classical reference is to Pompey, Crassus, and Caesar of the Roman Empire. Among such notables, David Thompson was lucky to appear in a footnote.

Following their trip in the fall of 1626, the Pilgrim leaders dropped David and his newly purchased trade goods back at Pannaway. There he disappears from our view. He reportedly died at Boston Harbor, some time between 1627 and 1628. One genealogy website pins his demise as December 13, 1628, a suspiciously precise and unsupported date. Thompson's cause of death is often listed as an accidental drowning, which is reasonable, but unproven. Few seventeenth-century citizens, fishermen included, ever learned to swim. Barring the discovery of a revealing long-lost document, we will never know when, where, or how New Hampshire's founder met his end.

Countless early American colonists were simply swallowed up by the vast continent. Sir Walter Raleigh left a hundred men and women on Roanoke Island (now North Carolina) in 1587. A return expedition thirteen years later found no trace of them. Likewise, no one knows what happened to the ten men Christopher Levett left at his outpost at Casco Bay, Maine in 1624.

In his 1873 history of the Isles of Shoals, John Scribner Jenness ticked down a list of seventeenth-century fishermen who fell out of their boats and drowned, were caught in sudden squalls, or froze to death. Towns up and down the New England coast are dotted with brass plaques and granite monuments to the hundreds of men and women lost at sea. Rather than puzzle over Thompson's fate, let us review what happened to two of his contemporaries. Thomas Morton, best known for dancing around an eighty-foot high maypole, offers a cautionary tale about what happens when you antagonize the Pilgrim fathers. We'll tackle his story in an upcoming chapter. Roger Conant, by contrast, managed to adapt to Puritan control and founded the town of Salem.

Baptized in Devonshire in 1592, Roger Conant was the same age as David Thompson. Worthington Ford, an early twentieth-century Pilgrim scholar, has even suggested that Conant came to New England with Thompson aboard the *Jonathan* in 1623. By 1624, Conant and his family were living as independent strangers among the saints of New Plymouth. Opposed to the harsh Separatist principles, Conant moved to Nantasket (now Hull) not far from where Thompson would soon claim his island in Boston Bay.

By 1625, the year David Thompson wrote his letter to the Earl of Arundel, Roger Conant was managing a fishing outpost at Cape Ann, now part of the Massachusetts North Shore. Founded in 1623 by

English investors from Dorchester, the Cape Ann fishing settlement was in trouble from the start. Not only was it unprofitable, but due to overlapping charters, the Pilgrims and another group claimed title to the same land. The resulting dispute offers another tantalizing hint about Thompson's brief time in America.

William Bradford, documents reveal, initially had high hopes of setting up a fishing operation on Cape Ann. The New Plymouth group even built a staging site to dry cod there. In a 1623 letter back to English investors, Bradford wrote that ". . . fishing must be the chief, if not the only means to do us good, and [Cape Ann] is like to be so fit a place, and lyeth so near us; we think it very necessary to use all diligence to procure it." Bradford wrote this in September, mere months after Thompson delivered his fish to the starving Pilgrims.

But as we noted earlier, the Pilgrims were not fishermen. Bradford's struggling group never got its fishing operation off the ground at Cape Ann. The Dorchester Company also made a poor start at Cape Ann and, by 1625, following three unsatisfactory harvests, they were pulling out. Here the plot thickens. That same year, without requesting permission from the Pilgrims, another fishing expedition used the Cape Ann staging to salt and dry their catch. Bradford, who by this time had a patent for Cape Ann from the Council, sent hot-tempered Miles Standish to confront the fishing group led by Captain John Hewes. The meeting almost erupted into bloodshed. According to legend, Roger Conant, who had moved from New Plymouth to Cape Ann, was able to negotiate a truce between Miles Standish and the fishermen led by Captain Hewes. Standish's hostile treatment of the fishermen so angered the Pilgrim's London investors that they filed a complaint. The Separatists, they argued, were "contentious, cruel and hard-hearted against your neighbors. . . [who] jump not with you."

How does David Thompson fit into this story? In a 2013 doctoral thesis for Northeastern University, Sean Delaney noted that Bradford once named both David Thompson and Thomas Weston as possible competitors for a patent to Cape Ann. Neither man was considered a friend of New Plymouth. Based on his 1625 letter home, it appears Thompson was at Cape Ann during this potentially explosive moment.

Thompson wrote that he "hardly escaped great murder and bloodshed at Cape Ann." Sixteen or seventeen musketeers from New Plymouth appeared at the fishing outpost, he reported to the Earl of Arundel. "By good fortune, I was there accidentally, and used many arguments on both sides to dissuade such ungodly, violent and unanswerable proceedings." Was it David Thompson and not Roger Conant who brokered the peace between Captain Hewes' fishermen and the thin-skinned Miles Standish? The evidence is compelling.

Discouraged by poor fishing seasons, the Dorchester Company gave up their experiment entirely in 1626—the same year David Thompson gave up on Pannaway. The company offered Cape Ann fishing families free passage back to England. But, like the Thompsons, Conant and his family elected to give New England a second chance. Conant and a dozen fishermen set up a colony originally known as Naumkeag, now Salem. The name comes from *shalom*, a Jewish word that translates to peacefulness, wholeness, completeness, and safety. The modern cities of Peabody, Beverly, and Danvers were originally part of Salem.

Roger Conant traded in fishing for farming. David Thompson, meanwhile, was setting up his new operation at a fertile spot that Natives had been farming for centuries. But here the two lives diverge. Conant lived a long life in a large house with an expansive family. He went on to serve in every civic role imaginable from governor of Salem to juror and judge. In 1913, his descendants funded an imposing nine-foot-tall bronze sculpture of Roger Conant. Mounted on a sixty-ton granite boulder, dressed in a dark flowing cloak and wide-brimmed Puritan hat, it faces Salem Commons today. Unfortunately, it is located next to the city's Witch Museum, giving tourists the false impression that Conant was either a Pilgrim, a member of the Salem Witch Trials, or a warlock.

Clifford Shipton, Conant's biographer, politely described sculptor Henry Kitson's choice of Puritan costume as "debatable." Shipton assembled his life of Conant from scattered, occasionally sketchy, references. Like David Thompson, Conant is considered, at best, a minor character in the founding of New England. But after years of study, Shipton found his subject to be "a solid, useful, gentle, honorable man," unlike many of his contemporaries.

In his short story "Main Street," Nathaniel Hawthorne had only good words for the founder of Salem. "Roger Conant is of that class of men," Hawthorne wrote, "who do not merely find, but make their place in the system of human affairs." Had David Thompson lived, he too might be remembered among the rugged "old planters" of Boston.

CHAPTER 20
Amias Weds Samuel

We know a great deal more about Amias Thompson's second husband than about her first. Samuel Maverick, son of an Episcopalian minister and a firm Royalist was born in England in 1602, making him about five years younger than his wife. He may have arrived among the settlers brought by Governor Robert Gorges and abandoned near Wessagusset. Others suggest he came over in 1623 to join Captain Christopher Levett's survey of Maine. Maverick appears to have owned land in both locations.

Samuel Maverick features in modern Massachusetts tour guides as a prosperous merchant who was "key to the commercial success of colonial Boston." He is often listed as the first documented resident of East Boston, even though, once again, the region had been occupied by indigenous people for millennia. Early accounts differ, but we can piece together a workable timeline to explain how Amias and Samuel became a couple.

By 1624, Samuel Maverick was living at Winnisimmet, now the city of Chelsea. If we accept that the Thompsons moved to Thompson Island in 1626 or even 1627, then they were living a quick sail away from Noddles Island (also Noddle's), where Maverick later set up a trading post. Whether Maverick had visited the Thompsons at Pannaway, either through Governor Gorges or Captain Levett, we do not know, but it seems they briefly lived on neighboring islands when in Boston.

Edward Johnson, an early member of the Great Migration of Puritans to Massachusetts, offered this intriguing comment: "On this Island [Noddles] he [Maverick] had built a small fort with the help of one Mr. David Thompson, placing therein four murtherers to protect him from the Indians." Maverick's murtherers, or "murdering pieces," according to an early dictionary, were small brass or iron cannons charged with nails and bits of iron. They were chiefly used on ships to "clear the decks" when boarded by an enemy.

Whether Thompson helped Maverick build his first house on the mainland at Winnisimmet or on Noddles Island depends on who is telling the story. In some accounts, Maverick gets the island by marrying Amias or by purchasing it with her money.

It doesn't take a giant leap of logic, even for a historian, to suggest that the Thompsons and Maverick were acquainted before David died in 1627 or 1628. Both men were Anglicans, not Puritans, and both held patents from the Council for New England. The marriage between Amias and Samuel is widely listed as 1628, not unreasonable considering that Widow Thompson was suddenly alone in the wilderness with a child.

As heir to her first husband's patent for an island and a portion of 6,000 acres, Amias was arguably the wealthiest English woman in New England. Noddles Island, it has been suggested, was among her real estate holdings. The name, according to legend, came from adventurer William Noddle, who joined a 1602 expedition that had visited the region almost twenty years before the *Mayflower*. Situated close to the mainland, Noddles has since been filled in and partially absorbed by Boston Logan International Airport.

The Mavericks were certainly established on Noddles Island in 1629. The following year Reverend John Winthrop's fleet of eleven ships delivered 700 Puritan immigrants to New England. This was the first wave of the Massachusetts Bay Colony movement. Thousands more would soon follow. Captain Edward Johnson, mentioned above, was among the landing party at Boston Harbor, a historic moment that would impact the character of the future United States more than the Pilgrim landing ten years earlier. Johnson says Winthrop first set foot in Boston Harbor at Noddles Island. His host, Mr. Maverick, Johnson reported, was "a man of a very loving and courteous behavior, very ready to entertain strangers, yet an enemy to the reformation in hand, being strong for the lordly prelatical power."

Maverick, in other words, was of the Anglican or Episcopal faith. His religion included high-ranking Christian leaders known as "prelates" or bishops. Puritan reformers were opposed to these powerful bishops who could appoint church ministers. Puritans, in their efforts to "purify" the Christian faith, believed in electing their own ministers from within each separate church congregation. As friendly as Maverick may have appeared on the surface, his allegiance to King Charles and to the Church of England was as threatening to the Puritans moving into Boston as David Thompson had been to the Pilgrims of New Plymouth. Eventually, Maverick and his family would be driven out of the area.

John Winthrop, an English lawyer, is best known today for a 1630 speech he delivered either while departing for New England or soon after his arrival. Quoting scripture, Winthrop warned his followers that their new Puritan nation would be "as a city upon a hill, the eyes of all people are upon us." Their experimental society in New England, he warned his fellow immigrants, would succeed or fail based on their strict adherence to Puritan principles. Winthrop's speech, known as "A Model of Christian Charity," was rediscovered in the early nineteenth century even as many Americans became familiar with the legends of pious Pilgrims landing at Plymouth Rock. President Ronald Reagan often likened the United States to "a shining city on a hill." The phrase is often connected to the concept of American exceptionalism, a theory that the United States was uniquely founded as a republic. The term is often confused with the belief that the nation is somehow superior to other countries.

Countless politicians have invoked Winthrop's catchphrase. A young Senator Barack Obama, for instance, used it while campaigning in Boston in 2006. Obama said:

> *It was right here, in the waters around us, where the American experiment began. As the earliest settlers arrived on the shores of Boston and Salem and Plymouth, they dreamed of building a City upon a Hill.*

Unlike her male counterparts, Amias Cole Thompson Maverick gets no respect. She scarcely appears in the history of either New Hampshire or Massachusetts. And yet, she witnessed the founding of New England from an unprecedented point of view. Through her father and first husband, she was connected to Sir Ferdinando Gorges as he struggled to carve out an Anglican colony in America. She may have met Captain John Smith and Captain John Mason while living in England. Arriving here, she hosted Standish, Winslow, and Bradford—the three best known passengers from the *Mayflower*—at her home in Little Harbor. There she welcomed Thomas Weston, Christopher Levett, Robert Gorges and others to Pannaway. And she met "the father of Massachusetts Bay" as John Winthrop arrived in Boston aboard the Puritan flagship *Arabella* in 1630. Winthrop would govern the new colony with an iron fist for twelve of its first twenty years. No woman of the era had a more in-depth view of the birth of New England.

1630 was a watershed year. In the coming decade, an estimated 20,000 Puritans, half from the East Anglia region of England, would follow in Winthrop's footsteps. It became, for Puritan historians, a holy exodus of biblical significance. Alexander Young, author of the once widely read *Chronicles of the Pilgrim Fathers* (1844), listed settlements begun by David Thompson, Thomas Weston, and Robert Gorges as merely "abortive attempts" to plant an English colony. The only successful colony prior to Massachusetts Bay was New Plymouth.

"As for the rest of the plantations, they were like the habitations of the foolish, as it is in Job, cursed before they had taken root," Young noted with authority. "But the vanishing of all the aforementioned attempts did but make way for settling the Colony of Massachusetts." Not even the Pilgrims could match Winthrop's city on a hill, as Young and countless others claimed, because the Massachusetts Bay Colony, they believed, was ordained by God.

Besides settlers and a patent for the colony of Massachusetts, John Winthrop's fleet carried swine, goats, sheep, and horses. The Puritans brought nails, glass, and ironwork for building. And they came prepared with weapons, gunpowder, and bullets. The first Puritan wave, according to English traveler John Josselyn, cost a whopping 192,000 British pounds, around $50 million today.

"They [Puritans] set down first upon Noddles Island," Josselyn wrote, "and afterward, they began to build upon the main." Technically, Josselyn's account is misleading. The Puritans initially landed at Naumkeag, later Salem, but soon moved south to what would become Boston Bay. Josselyn visited with the Mavericks in 1638. As we'll see in the next chapter, he later described an event at the Maverick home so horrific and scandalous that it is still being talked about today.

But in 1630, Amias and Samuel Maverick were preparing for the birth of their first of three children. In future Charlestown and along the Boston waterfront, the homes of the "Great Puritan Migration" were springing up. Meanwhile, back on the Piscataqua River, a mining and trading colony known as Strawberry Bank was off to a rocky start.

CHAPTER 21
The Mavericks' Journey

It wasn't until 1893 that Portsmouth history buff Frank W. Hackett made a surprising connection. Amias Maverick and Amias Thompson were the same person. "The mystery is solved," a researcher from England wrote in response to Hackett's genealogical inquiry. "You need to have no doubt of the identity. . . It is one of the most curious coincidences in my experience."

The clues were hidden in a letter written in 1635 by Amias Maverick of Noddles Island (spelled "Nottles") in Massachusetts. She addressed her note to Robert Trelawny, a merchant in Plymouth, England. The message was polite, but desperate.

"I am given to understand . . ." Mrs. Maverick wrote, "that my father is very much incensed against me." Amias had received word her father, William Cole, was about to sell off a plot of land in Plymouth, England that he had previously promised to his daughter. Amias planned to give the property to her children, perhaps indicating she and Samuel were considering a return to England. Amias begged Trelawny to convince her father not to sell the land.

Her only known letter did not mention shipwright Cole by name. But eagle-eyed Frank Hackett, a lawyer by trade, noticed Amias' mention of her "fatherless children," a possible reference to her son John in America and to her daughter Priscilla in England. Amias implored Trelawny for his help, "as you loved my first husband." Could the widowed Amias of Boston Bay, Hackett wondered, be the

1623 pioneer from Little Harbor? A journey through church records by a researcher in England closed the case. Her letter ended with a hand-drawn "merchant's mark," a seal that might represent her father, William Cole, or possibly Trelawny.

The two Thompsons, their only surviving letters prove, had friends in high places. In 1625, David had written to the famous art collector Thomas Howard, Earl of Arundel. Ten years later, Amias was emboldened to ask for a personal favor from Robert Trelawny, who was elected mayor of Plymouth three times before serving as a member of the British Parliament. The myth that the Thompsons only "came to fish" in New Hampshire doesn't hold water. They had bigger plans.

The timing of her letter home makes sense. By 1635, Amias and Samuel had three young children—Nathaniel, Samuel, and newborn Mary. Perhaps the Mavericks hoped to return to England. They were definitely aware of the value of real estate. Samuel owned land grants at Agamenticus (York) in Maine and 1,000 acres at Winnisimmet (Chelsea). Amias was potentially heir to her late husband's Piscataqua claims. Through his wife, Mr. Maverick had received an official title to Noddles Island from the Massachusetts General Court. He was also authorized to operate the nation's first ferry, running from Chelsea to North Boston. Their union made the Mavericks among the wealthiest New Englanders.

Considered hospitable to all, the Mavericks are credited with assisting a Native tribe stricken with smallpox. In his 1633 journal, Puritan leader John Winthrop remarked how Samuel, his wife, and their servants volunteered their services to the Indians. Amias "went daily to them, ministered to their necessities, and buried their dead, and took home many of their children," Winthrop wrote.

In 1635, Samuel made a successful business trip to Virginia. He stayed almost a year, leaving Amias and her servants to run the Noddles Island household and manage their children. He returned with two purchased ships "laden with corn" plus heifers and goats.

But Maverick's business success, his loyalty to the Crown and the Anglican Church, plus his reputation for hospitality to "all comers," made his Puritan neighbors nervous. Who was he entertaining? What was he doing on that island? The General Court ordered Maverick to move to Boston and not to lodge any visitors for more than one night. He seems to have ignored the demands of the Court and was briefly jailed in 1641.

One Puritan historian assumes, apparently based on Maverick's gregarious reputation, that he was a "hard-drinking" man. From Maverick's view, he was being harassed by religious fanatics who openly defied the Crown. In 1646, he signed a petition with other non-Puritans requesting his full civil rights as an English "freeman" and permission to operate a separate church. It was the wrong time to take on the rapidly expanding Massachusetts Bay Colony. Back in England, King Charles I was beheaded in 1649 and Oliver Cromwell, the "Puritan Moses" became Lord Protector of the Commonwealth.

Today, Samuel Maverick is frequently cited as the first Massachusetts "slave owner," a term now rightfully being retired from use. He may have been introduced to the sight of enslaved Africans while on business in Virginia. On January 26, 1638, Governor John Winthrop recorded the ship *Desire* had arrived in Boston from Bermuda. It "brought some cotton, and tobacco, and Negroes," he reported in his journal.

Samuel Maverick kept two enslaved African women and one young man. Travel writer John Josselyn happened to be staying with the Mavericks on Noddles Island in the fall of 1638. Josselyn had come from England to visit his brother Henry. Like Maverick and David Thompson, Henry Josselyn was an agent of Sir Ferdinando Gorges with dreams of establishing a successful plantation in New England.

John Josselyn called Maverick "the only hospitable man in all the country." And yet, at about 9:00 on the morning of October 2, Josselyn wrote, "Mr. Maverick's Negro woman" came to his window. She was distraught, loud and shrill, and speaking in her native tongue. Josselyn went to Maverick to learn why the African woman, who had reportedly been a queen in her own country, was so upset.

Maverick explained, he wanted to create "a breed of Negroes." He had commanded a young enslaved male "to go to bed to her," whether she wanted him or not. The woman had resisted, then afterwards, thrown the man out. "This she took in high disdain beyond her slavery, and this was the cause of her grief," Maverick told Josselyn. His effort to breed enslaved servants—a practice common among Revolutionary War-era founders—certainly negates Maverick's reputation as hospitable to all.

Neither Maverick nor Josselyn left any further record of the woman, but the evidence was clear. Within two decades of the arrival of Christians from Europe, chattel slavery was becoming part of New England culture. Indians captured in the Pequot War, meanwhile, were shipped as slaves to the West Indies, sold for sugar or traded for enslaved men, women, and children kidnapped from Africa. By 1641, slavery was legal in Massachusetts. By the end of the seventeenth century, 1,000 Africans were living in bondage there. Half a million Blacks were enslaved in the United States by the American Revolution, four million by the Civil War.

In her book *New England Bound (2016)*, Princeton history professor and Pulitzer Prize finalist Wendy Warren recounts the rape of Maverick's slave. "This woman's life deserves to be reconstructed simply because too many factors have conspired to make that reconstruction nearly impossible," Warren has written.

"Brought against her will to a foreign continent populated by peoples speaking unfamiliar languages, sold as property, raped, and then ignored in the public record, her story mirrors that of millions,"

Warren explains. It is a narrative largely missing, until now, of a region best known as the cradle of American democracy and religious freedom.

The early colonization of New England "was a time of warfare and brutality and a lot of fear and trauma," Warren told reporter Terry Gross in a radio interview about her book. "Do you think that Americans need to constantly re-evaluate who we are as Americans and how our history was built?" the radio host asked the historian.

"It would be great," Warren replied, "if we understood that slavery was there right from the beginning, that it was embedded in the process of colonization, that in some cases it drove the process of colonization." And as Maverick proves, that was true in both northern and southern colonies.

But the Maverick story doesn't end there. We know that John Thompson, with his stepfather's help, gained ownership of Thompson Island in 1648. By then, Samuel Maverick had been prosecuted (he said "persecuted") by the Puritan court for his pro-Anglican petition. Driven out of Massachusetts by 1650, he reappears back in England a decade later. By this time, Oliver Cromwell was dead and King Charles II was on the throne. Amias, then in her sixties, likely stayed behind. Her daughter, Mary Maverick, was married to the successful Francis Hooke of Kittery, Maine. Amias appears to have been living in the vicinity, not far from her landing site at Little Harbor across the Piscataqua River.

For Maverick, the restoration of the English monarchy from Puritan control must have felt like payback. His 1660 publication, *A Description of New England*, was an encyclopedic guide to eighty-six coastal towns in America. Most had sprung up since he joined the "first planters" in 1624. Most of the towns he described, from Maine to Connecticut, are familiar today. In New Hampshire, for example, Maverick listed Exeter, Hampton, Dover, Oyster River (Durham) and Strawberry Bank (Portsmouth) on the Piscataqua River.

The author paused in the middle of his tour to complain about

Puritan governance. Like Thomas Morton and Ferdinando Gorges before him, Maverick had hoped to find a legal method to overturn the oppressive leaders of Massachusetts Bay through the English courts. Under Governor Winthrop, he explained, only men who renounced the Church of England and joined the Puritan congregation could vote, participate in local government, receive communion, or baptize their children. Anyone who dared protest that "arbitrary tyranny," was subject to fines and imprisonment. To even question the oppressive laws, Maverick well knew, was to invite banishment like so many before him.

Maverick reported that Massachusetts was melting down British coins to create its own currency. Men above age sixteen were required to sign a loyalty oath to support the colony above their king. Missing a church service led to a five pence fine. Not contributing to the salary of the local minister could result in a public whipping. The Puritans had even torn down the British flag, calling the iconic English Red Cross "a badge of the whore of Babylon." Three Quakers had been hanged in Boston for practicing their peaceful worship. This was not the society of people espousing religious freedom for anyone other than themselves, Maverick warned.

The manuscript for *A Description of New England* remained in private hands until the British Museum purchased it at auction in 1875. Ten years later, it was published by the Massachusetts Historical Society. It has slowly become an accepted alternative to the dominant Puritan history of the region.

Like David Thompson, Maverick claimed the early English colonies were too small, too weak, and spread too far apart to remain safe from Indian attack. As a result, he lived to see town after town fall under Massachusetts protection and control. Maverick didn't have a kind word for the Brownists of New Plymouth or the Puritans who followed them. Having come to America "to enjoy liberty of Conscience," he wrote, they then denied the same to everyone else.

Appointed as one of four royal commissioners by King Charles II, Samuel Maverick left England and returned to America in 1664, forty years after his first visit. His efforts to investigate complaints in New England and to reign in Puritan power were entirely unsuccessful. There was no stopping Puritan domination of the region. Assigned to reduce the Dutch presence in New York, he was living on the "Broad Way" in 1669 and presumed dead by the following year.

The demise of John Thompson, David's son, is equally foggy. According to *The Thompson Family* (1913), John lost his claim to Thompson Island in 1657. He reappeared as a founding citizen of the town of Mendon in 1662, married Sarah (dates and surname unknown), and died at Mendon in 1685. A will leaves his estate to an only son, John Thompson, Jr., from whom modern descendants claim their connection to New Hampshire's founding couple. Maybe not.

Aware that the Thompson name was common in early New England, the authors of *The Thompson Family*, made their genealogical case from among a cluster of John Thompsons. Their book was published by the Mendon Historical Society where one John Thompson lived. A more recent theory contends David Thompson's only son was in London by the 1650s. This John Thompson claimed, during a court case, that he was the owner of Thompson Island in New England who later forfeited his property due to an unpaid debt. The whereabouts of this John Thompson are unknown after 1652. If he was the true son of David and Amias, then no direct descendants of the couple are known.

Amias Thompson Maverick outlived two husbands and most of her children. In 1672, her son Nathaniel Maverick of Barbados mentioned his mother in his will. She reportedly died that year while living in Saco, Maine, just shy of her fiftieth year in New England.

V. MISCONCEPTIONS

"Many things which are false are transmitted from book to book and gain credit in the world."

 — The Life of Samuel Johnson *by James Boswell, 1791*

"Good history upsets everyone."

 — *Historian David Silverman* from an interview in National Geographic, *2020*

"How easy it is to make people believe a lie, and [how] hard it is to undo that work again!"

 — *Mark Twain, dictating his autobiography in 1906*

CHAPTER 22
We're on Our Way Home

So ends the tale of David and Amias Thompson and, having set the record straight, we could drop it here. But there's a problem. By delivering the facts about New Hampshire's founding family, we have knocked the traditional narrative of New England off-kilter. It's easy to recount the happy Thanksgiving legend of 1621 without ever mentioning Wessagusset, but the 1623 massacre is central to the Thompson story.

Sir Ferdinando Gorges, an essential figure in early efforts to colonize New England, is barely mentioned in the Pilgrim narrative. Yet, behind the scenes, Gorges and his associates, David Thompson among them, saw the zealots of New Plymouth as a hindrance to building a profitable English kingdom in America.

The Thompson story also rewrites local history to include non-Puritans, merchant adventurers, indentured workers, people of color, and a host of desperate souls. In the words of historian and archaeologist Brian Fagan, "New England was settled, not by Pilgrims escaping persecution in a land peopled by Native Americans, but by roistering cod fishermen schooled in the rough-and-ready world of the migrant fishery."

Prying the lid off the Thompson story after 400 years has revealed a time when the American experiment might have gone a very different way. No one represents that moment better than Thomas Morton, whose one-man battle with the Pilgrims and Puritans deserves at least its own chapter. In 1628, the likely year of Thompson's death, Miles Standish was abandoning Morton alone on the Isles of Shoals without food, tools, or shelter.

That same year, not far away, Edward Hilton was building a trading post at what would become Dover Point on the Piscataqua River. At Boston Bay, Amias and Samuel Maverick were setting up housekeeping. In England, with the cessation of foreign wars, the reanimated Council for New England was about to issue a burst of land grants, including one to the Laconia Company and Captain John Mason.

Another joint stock group, the one that would change the world as we know it, was about to stake its claim. In 1628, King Charles I granted the Charter of the Massachusetts Bay Company. John Winthrop, the group's wealthiest member, was appointed governor. The Company would come to dominate the regional government while the graduates of Harvard College (founded in 1636) shaped the culture of New England. Outliers like Thompson, Maverick, Gorges, Mason, Morton, and others were largely brushed aside by historians who followed.

On March 2, 1629, annoyed by members of the House of Commons who had "given themselves over to faction" both political and religious, Charles I dissolved Parliament for the next eleven years. With their new patent in hand, John Winthrop and thousands of Puritans figured it was high time to set up their own largely independent British satellite across the sea. But Puritan domination was not yet guaranteed. That same year, Sir Ferdinando Gorges married his fourth wife, a wealthy widow who was also his cousin. With enough income to give up his command at Plymouth, Gorges refocused his resources on colonizing New England. The land about to be occupied by Puritans, he believed, already belonged to him.

But first things first. Exiled by both Pilgrim and Puritan leaders, demeaned by early historians, Thomas Morton is back. "During his life," according to University of Southern California's Peter C. Mancall,

"Morton promoted a different path to colonization." Mancall's book-length study, *The Trials of Thomas Morton* (2016), reveals Morton's alternative to Puritan rule was in full bloom during David Thompson's brief time in America. In the pages we have left, after visiting Morton at Merry Mount, we have just enough space to reexamine the legend of Hilton's Point and tackle a few common misconceptions about the settlement at Strawberry Bank. Then we will briefly examine how the 1623 date spawned a history of seacoast celebrations that largely ignore its first English family.

CHAPTER 23
The Thomas Morton Affair

A single leaf of paper supports the theory that Thompson was dead by early 1628. The reference comes, once more, from Governor William Bradford, who preserved a collection of letters and documents dated between 1624 and 1630. After his death, *Governor Bradford's Letter Book* passed through the hands of early colonial ministers and historians. Like other documents that disappeared during the American Revolution, fragments resurfaced after the war. Bradford's letters were found in a Nova Scotia grocer's shop, then edited and published.

The correspondence that interests us was written by Bradford and sent to Sir Ferdinando Gorges in England. Bradford's strongly worded letter, dated June 15, 1628, asked Gorges and the Council for New England to remove and punish one Thomas Morton. An English lawyer, poet, and adventurer born around 1575, Morton visited New Plymouth briefly in 1622. He returned in 1624 to set up his own very different style colony. Morton adopted a trading post initially named for Richard Wollaston, possibly a pirate of whom little is known, who brought thirty indentured servants. Wollaston quickly left for Virginia and Morton turned the settlement, situated a few leagues from Plymouth Colony, into a successful Indian trading post. Dubbed Mare Mount ("a hill by the sea") the site is part of modern day Quincy on Boston Bay.

Mare Mount, better known as Merry Mount, offered a laid-back lifestyle that reportedly offended the Pilgrims. Its colonists were fond of celebrating, drinking, and mixing with the Natives. In a tradition common in medieval England, they raised an eighty-foot-tall maypole topped with deer antlers. They danced around the maypole in what Morton called "harmless mirth." Pilgrim leaders had seen maypoles, a symbol of merry Old England, employed at the fishing outposts of Monhegan and Damariscove, but not in their own backyard.

Worse, Bradford wrote to Gorges, Morton was accused of selling guns to the Indians. The guns, by all accounts, were used exclusively for protection and hunting. This allowed the Indians to hunt more efficiently and secure more furs. Their success, in turn, made Merry Mount the most profitable trading post in the region.

It has been suggested that Morton's greatest threat to New Plymouth was economic, not moral, social, or military. By befriending the Natives instead of murdering them as Standish had done, Morton's traders were becoming serious competitors to New Plymouth. According to Emerson Baker, a history professor at Salem State University, Morton's business success extended to the territory of Maine. "In 1625 or 1627, he sailed a vessel up the Kennebec and bought all the Indian furs before Plymouth's agents even arrived to trade," Baker writes. "Morton's success in the fur trade made Plymouth all the more eager to deport him."

Although Governor Bradford blamed Morton for arming the Natives and having "taught them the use of pieces," the practice had been carried on for at least two decades by French, Dutch, and English fishermen and explorers. Local Natives, Bradford estimated, owned up to sixty guns, although how many Morton may have sold is unknown. And while the Pilgrims were understandably nervous about armed indigenous neighbors, historians point out that the matchlock rifle was a tricky machine. Once charged with powder, the gun was fired by a slow burning wick. An expert marksman could shoot no more than three rounds per minute, assuming the weather was dry. Trained warriors, meanwhile, were capable of highly accurate and rapid fire with bows and arrows.

Morton welcomed indentured men and servants as equals at his colony. This practice struck at the English caste system that forced many to live in servitude and poverty. "Besides, they saw they should keep no servants," Bradford reported to Gorges, "for Morton would entertain any, how vile soever, and all the scum of the country, or any discontents, would flock to him of all places, if this nest were not broken." Two decades later, Samuel Maverick, who married David Thompson's widow, would also be accused of sheltering undesirable visitors at his home in Boston Bay.

Gorges, of course, had no love for the religious extremists of New Plymouth, which may be why Bradford warned that Morton was a threat to all settlers throughout the region, including Anglicans. "And they [New Englanders] should stand in more fear of their lives and goods in a short time from this wicked and debased crew than from the savages themselves," Bradford wrote in the summer of 1628. David Thompson had issued a similar warning three years earlier in his letter to the Earl of Arundel, but without naming Morton.

To support his claim that Morton, "the Lord of Misrule," was the most dangerous person on the continent, Bradford either convinced or coerced the leaders of the lesser "struggling plantations" to contribute to a fund. It has been described as New England's first tax. The pooled money was to pay Morton's passage back to England before he and his consorts "grew to further head and strength."

These contributing plantations, preserved in *Governor Bradford's Letter Book,* provide a snapshot of New England five years after the Thompsons arrived. We find a brief analysis of the list by none other than the Pulitzer Prize-winning Harvard historian Samuel Eliot Morison, whose edition of Bradford's *Of Plymouth Plantation* appeared in 1952. Morison is best known in Portsmouth as the author of a definitive 1959 biography of John Paul Jones and as an early advisor to Strawbery Banke Museum.

Bradford's list is a critical document. The settlements aligned to banish Morton included Roger Conant at Naumkeag (Salem), the survivors of Robert Gorges' colony at Wessagusset (Weymouth), Reverend William Blackstone at Shawmut (Boston), Edward Hilton (at Dover Point), the unnamed planters living at Pascataquack (Little Harbor), and colonists at Natascot (Hull). The smallest contribution—but most significant to us here—came from "Mrs. Thompson." Morrison referred to her as "the widow Thompson of Thompson's Island."

Not only is it surprising to see a widowed mother being, in effect, publicly taxed by the leaders of New Plymouth, but the inference is clear—David was dead. Amias Thompson was apparently not yet married to Samuel Maverick, who is conspicuously missing from Bradford's list. Equally revealing is that someone at Pannaway, we know not who, was able to kick in the hefty fee of two pounds and ten shillings, a sum matched only by the Pilgrims and by the settlers at Salem. Edward Hilton, who appears on the record for the first time at Dover Point in 1628, contributed one pound sterling, while Amias Thompson could only spare fifteen shillings.

Novelist and American literature professor William Heath paints Morton as "an aristocrat by birth and a bon vivant by inclination. . . he was fond of falconry and foppery, bawdy puns and esoteric poetry. . . He was, in sum, an Elizabethan dandy, a man of the Renaissance, with a smattering of high culture, and a hankering for low adventure." Journalist Carleton Beals described Morton as a man in love with everything he encountered in America, and whose delight in the beauty and bounty around him shone in sharp contrast to "the dour misgivings" of the *Mayflower* Pilgrims.

Anticipating his arrest, Thomas Morton turned himself in. The hot-tempered Miles Standish wanted to execute Morton on the spot, but cooler heads prevailed. Pilgrim leaders informed Morton that selling guns and powder to the Natives was forbidden by a proclamation issued years earlier by King James I. A trained lawyer from a prominent family, Morton pointed out, "Proclamations are no laws and enforce no penalties." Besides, he added sarcastically, "The King is dead, and his displeasure with him."

Standish transported his prisoner by shallop to the Isles of Shoals, which was then empty of its seasonal fishing teams. Morton was stranded there, he later wrote, "without gun, powder, or shot, or dog or so much as a knife to get anything to feed upon." Dressed only in a single suit of clothes, he lingered on one of the nine islands for a month, possibly longer. His only help, Morton wrote, came from Natives who arrived by canoe and "would bring bottles of strong liquor. . . and unite themselves into a league of brotherhood."

Morton eventually caught a ride back to England aboard a fishing ship. Sir Ferdinando Gorges ignored Bradford's claim that Morton was a "pettifogger" who had consorted with Indian women, sold guns to Natives, and ran a "School for Atheism." No trial was held in England and no punishment assessed. In 1629, the year following his banishment, Morton boldly returned to New England to again run his outpost at Mare Mount.

But Thomas Morton's reputation made him an automatic enemy to the incoming leader of Massachusetts Bay. Governor John Winthrop saw Morton as the serpent in their new Garden of Eden and a dark cloud over his shining city on a hill. Puritan forces soon arrested Morton. They seized his property, chopped down his new maypole, and burned his house. Morton's crime—a trumped up charge—was stealing a canoe from an Indian and suspicion of a murder back in England. Shipped back across the sea, the now middle-aged lawyer combined forces with Sir Ferdinando Gorges. Together, they worked to revoke the charters for New Plymouth and Massachusetts Bay Colony through the English courts. For the Separatists and the Puritan leaders of Massachusetts, Morton had evolved from a nuisance to a dangerous enemy.

In their battle to undermine the Puritans, Morton and Gorges joined with Captain John Mason, soon to be the founder of a new settlement on the Piscataqua called Strawberry Bank. The Separatists, they argued in a London court, had been issued a charter to settle in Virginia in 1620. Instead, they had illegally established a colony in a region chartered to Gorges. Pilgrim leader Edward Winslow was forced back to London to defend the New Plymouth land claim. Samuel Maverick later called Winslow "a smooth tongued cunning fellow."

Despite his potent legal case against New Plymouth, the aging Sir Ferdinando was running out of steam. While in Bristol, he was thrown from a horse and afterwards needed his servant's help to walk. Despite a windfall upon marrying his fourth wife, neither he nor the Council had the financial resources to mount a major military action. There was talk of raising a thousand men to eliminate what one historian called the "religious virus" infecting New England. But the Puritan migration was well underway and, all too soon, Gorges' partnership with Captain John Mason would end in tragedy.

When efforts to oust the two religious colonies from Massachusetts failed, Thomas Morton published a book. His *New English Canaan* (1637) continues to confuse, provoke, entertain, and inspire readers to this day. The title reference is to a Biblical legend of an ancient society destroyed by God for their idolatry. Divided into three sections, Morton's book first offered a rapturous description of the New England landscape, natural resources, plants, and animals. He then pictured the indigenous people he had met as hospitable, passionate, generous, and resourceful. The more time Morton spent among the civilized Indians, he wrote, the more savage his own countrymen appeared. Members of New England tribes, he added, were "more full of humanity than the Christians."

The third section of *New English Canaan* was a scathing attack on the harsh regime of the Separatists and the Massachusetts Bay Puritans. It is through Morton's satirical eye that Miles Standish became "Captain Shrimp." Massachusetts governor John Endicott, who could be hostile to anyone outside the Puritan circle, was parodied as "Captain Littleworth." It was Morton who dared label Standish's 1623 attack on Pecksuot, Wituwamat, and the other Indian warriors as the "massacre" at Wessagusset. And it was Morton who revealed that the Natives had come to know the Pilgrims as "stabbers" or "cutthroats."

Morton's version of the 1623 Indian assassinations closely follows the details offered by the Pilgrim leaders. But he did not believe the rumor—offered by both Massasoit and Phineas Pratt—that the Natives were secretly conspiring to wipe out both Weston's colony and New Plymouth. Without evidence and without a trial, Morton implied, there was no justification for the planned slaughter during what Standish had promised the Indians would be a peaceful meeting.

Printed in the Netherlands, banned in England, few copies of Morton's manifesto made it into private hands in America. Thanks to accounts by Bradford and Winthrop, Morton has gone down in history as a lawless, profiteering misfit. President John Adams and his son, President John Quincy Adams, were fascinated to learn that Morton's Mare Mount colony had been located on their family farm in Quincy.

Interest in Thomas Morton began to grow after Nathaniel Hawthorne's short story, "The May-Pole of Merry Mount" (1834) pictured him in a sympathetic light. Historian Charles Frances Adams, Jr. the grandson and great-grandson of two American presidents, also became fascinated by Morton. His carefully researched edition of *New English Canaan*, published in 1883, offered a more nuanced view of the activist lawyer and merchant adventurer. Modern studies have since begun to take Morton more seriously as a historian, even questioning the validity of Bradford's version of the Wessagusset murders.

Were Native warriors seriously planning to attack New Plymouth or just posturing? Did Captain Standish lose control over an insult? What did Massasoit have to gain from a Pilgrim attack on rival tribes? Was the raid, along with Morton's expulsion, designed to eliminate all competing Anglican trading posts? Was Morton's idea of a more liberal, socially progressive, and racially diverse America viable, or was he, as John Winthrop wrote, merely an "arrant knave"?

Ever reckless, after the publication of his book Thomas Morton traveled back to New Plymouth for the fourth time in 1642. He was quickly clapped in irons, denied a trial, and thrown in jail. Morton languished all winter in a Boston prison without a warming fire or bedding. Aging and ill, his spirit finally broken, Morton begged for clemency. Considered too weak and mentally unfit for further punishment, Morton was fined 100 pounds and released. Banished to the distant colony of Agamenticus (or Acomenticus), now York, Maine, he died in 1647. Thomas Jefferson, in a letter to John Adams, once noted that Morton, "being grown old in wickedness,at last ended his life at Piscataqua." His burial site is unknown.

Reviled by early Puritan scholars, Thomas Morton has become, for some historians, a revisionist anti-hero. He stands out as an eyewitness and victim of religious intolerance in Massachusetts. Morton had to be eliminated, but unlike Wituwamat, he could not be killed directly. Instead, he was banished, abandoned, fined, and imprisoned nearly to death. For Bradford, *New English Canaan* was an "infamous and scurrilous book against many godly and chief men of the country, full of lies and slanders." Samuel Maverick, however, praised Morton's work as "the truest description of New England as then it was that ever I saw."

The controversial Mr. Morton matters to us because, by his own words, he knew David Thompson. Thompson Island was situated just offshore from Mare Mount Colony. Their meeting, sometime between 1624 and 1628, was inevitable. In *New English Canaan*, Morton described Thompson and another man, Sir Christopher Gardiner, as "conversant" with the Natives. Gardiner appears in Governor Bradford's journal around 1630, accompanied by "a comely young woman whom he called his cousin," but the Pilgrims suspected she was Gardiner's concubine. Gardiner was later run out of town, no surprise, by the Puritans of Massachusetts Bay.

From the Separatist perspective, Gardiner, Thompson, Morton, and Maverick were all associates of Sir Ferdinando Gorges, possibly spies. From Morton's view, Thompson and Gardiner were "both scholars and travelers" who shared an interest in the lives of indigenous people. They were "diligent in taking notice of these things as men of good judgment." Morton's scholarship, however, led to his belief that the Natives of New England were descended from the ancient Greeks. We can only imagine Thompson and Morton, pipe and beer glass in hand, discussing their theories. At least one scholar has suggested the Thompsons and their neighbor, Samuel Maverick, were among the revelers who danced around the maypole at Merry Mount. The timeline and proximity make that vaguely possible, but unprovable.

There is also academic speculation that the "rich widow" Morton refers to in *New English Canaan* might be Amias Thompson. Couched in allusions to classical Greek mythology, Morton referenced Scylla and Charybdis, two sea monsters that were a danger to sailors. Once a beautiful woman, Scylla had six heads and six arms that she used to catch any fish or men who passed by her cave. Charybdis is sometimes depicted as a deadly whirlpool, swallowing up passing ships. Could this be a reference to David Thompson's death by drowning? Or does Morton's puzzling satire, rich with symbols of sexuality and fertility, refer to the marriage of the widowed Mrs. Thompson to her neighbor Samuel Maverick? Four centuries after the publication of *New English Canaan*, Morton's readers are still scratching their heads in confusion.

CHAPTER 24
Debunking the Hilton Claim

Before wrapping up the Thompson story, we must examine the long held claim that a second Piscataqua settlement was established in 1623 at what is now Dover. The legend began, as we've noted, when the Puritan government paid Congregational minister William Hubbard fifty pounds to compose *A General History of New England* (1680).

Born in Ipswich, England, Hubbard was a child when his parents emigrated with him to America. That would make him about seven years old when David Thompson died. Among the first graduates of Harvard College, Hubbard may have known the Hilton family. In his book, Hubbard specified that fishmongers Edward and William Hilton arrived at Little Harbor with Thompson. But he also noted that Thompson's house (which he incorrectly identified as "Mason Hall") was the first building in the region. He wrote, "The Hiltons, in the meanwhile, [were] setting up their stages higher up the river. . . at or about the place since called Dover."

We can scarcely imagine life in Hubbard's America as he composed his chronicle during the reign of Charles II, the Merry Monarch. Hubbard viewed his fragile young colony as England's "little sister which as yet hath no breasts." Massachusetts was just coming out of King Philip's War, a bloody conflict with indigenous people whom Hubbard called "the messengers of Satan."

To Hubbard, like so many historians who followed, civilization on the American continent began with the appearance of white Christians from England. Before that, "the inhabitants of that region sat in darkness and in the shadow of death," Hubbard wrote. The "discovery" and domination of the New World by Puritans, he firmly believed, was ordained by God. Hubbard's language regarding the Hilton settlement is vague. He identified the landing site only as "Dover," a term not used until at least 1637. Nor did he date the Hilton plantation to 1623, but only as "in the meanwhile."

Like so many of the errors in his book, it was a good guess. But in the words of New Hampshire Supreme Court Justice Elwin L. Page, "Hubbard set going a chain of guesses which have been written into New Hampshire history ever since." The Hilton claim, Page declared, is "provably erroneous."

A century after Hubbard, Reverend Jeremy Belknap adopted the same guesswork into his *History of New Hampshire* (1784) that appeared the year following the American Revolution. Much had changed since Hubbard compared local Natives to satanic messengers. In contrast, Belknap wrote:

> However fond we may have been of accusing the Indians of treachery
> and infidelity, it must be confessed that the example was first set
> them by the Europeans. Had we always treated them with that
> justice and humanity which our religion inculcates, and our true
> interest at all times required, we might have lived in as much
> harmony with them as with any other people on the globe.

Few worried about the identity of New Hampshire's first settlers until 1820, when Plymouth, Massachusetts, branded their Pilgrims as the forefathers of the United States. Serious debate arose in New Hampshire over whether the Thompsons or the Hiltons deserved the 1623 honors. The key resource was an 1813 reprint of Belknap's book. Renewed research suggested, however, that the Thompson settlement was clearly documented, while the Hilton claim was vague and speculative. The New Hampshire Historical Society, founded in 1823, later certified the Little Harbor outpost as "the first year-round English settlement in what became New Hampshire." Portsmouth, having once included the town of Rye, quickly claimed bragging rights, kicking off a quiet feud between Dover and Portsmouth that continues to this day.

Following three huge downtown fires and the War of 1812, Portsmouth's economy was in tatters. The city bicentennial of 1823 was a watershed moment. With the future uncertain, local historians began to dig into Portsmouth's fabled past. But even Nathaniel Adams (*Annals of Portsmouth*, 1825) and Charles W. Brewster (*Rambles About Portsmouth*, 1859) were limited to repeating the guesswork of their predecessors.

Dover historians, too, were doing their homework. Hubbard and Belknap, it turned out, were not infallible. Both had wrongly reported, for example, that Thompson spent only one year at Little Harbor before moving to Boston. That error was corrected in the 1831 edition of Belknap's book, edited by John Farmer, a founder of the New Hampshire Historical Society. Jeremy Belknap, it bears repeating, had been living in Dover for twenty years while writing his history. John Farmer was also from Dover, where his updated version of Belknap's book was published.

The discovery of David Thompson's 1622 indenture by Charles Deane rekindled the controversy in 1876. Deane could finally pinpoint a longstanding error dating back to 1680. William Hubbard had conflated a 1622 charter to John Mason and Ferdinando Gorges—a charter that was never acted on—with the grant of the same year to Thompson. Thompson's charter was with the Council for New England, and not with the Laconia Company, which was not even formed until after Thompson's death. It was the Laconia Company that gave the green light to John Mason's 1630 settlement at Strawberry Bank. The Thompson indenture, therefore, had no designs on planting a second settlement six or seven miles up the Piscataqua River as Hubbard,

Belknap, and almost everyone who followed them had claimed.

"We now know that this company [Thompson] had no interest in the settlement at Hilton's Point, afterwards Dover," Deane wrote. The Hilton colony, he said definitively, "came into existence at a later period."

What Deane said mattered. A history heavyweight, he had a special interest in the lesser-known founding tales of Maine and New Hampshire. Before his publication of the Thompson indenture, Deane had created the first authoritative catalog of the library at the Massachusetts Historical Society, where he served as vice president. Deane did his best work, according to a colleague, "with the most recondite, obscure, the tangled and perplexed elements and periods of our history."

Deane edited an edition of William Bradford's Plymouth journal and all the records of the Council for New England. He was an expert on the writings of Jeremy Belknap and Captain John Smith. Deane built a huge private library, keeping track of his painstaking research "on fly-leaves, margins, memoranda, and scraps of paper scattered between the pages of his 13,000 books." *Truth for truth's sake* was his motto.

William Hilton, contrary to Hubbard's theory, arrived at New Plymouth in 1621. He was followed in 1623 by his wife, Anne, and two children, when the couple received a tract of land from the Pilgrims. They lived in Massachusetts, possibly as late as 1627, Deane noted, before moving to Hilton's Point. Genealogical research places William briefly in Exeter before living in Kittery where he kept a tavern and ran a ferry. We later find him with a second wife in York, Maine. Records show him as the father of ten children, two of them named William.

Brother Edward, adding to the confusion, also had a son named William. The first official mention of Edward Hilton, Deane noted, was in 1628 when, according to William Bradford, Hilton contributed to the arrest and deportation of Thomas Morton of Merry Mount. Having set up a Piscataqua trading post in 1628, Edward appears to have returned to England where he received his charter from the Council for New England in 1630 (or March 1629 in the old-style Julian calendar). Deane argued that the charter in no way supports the theory that Edward had established himself in the region up to seven years before receiving his official patent.

In 1878, two years after Deane's article appeared, New York lawyer John Scribner Jenness delivered a stinging rebuttal of the Hilton claim. The son of a Portsmouth mayor, Jenness was a dogged researcher. His privately printed booklet, *Notes on the First Planting of New Hampshire (1878),* contained two beautifully inked and hand-colored maps of colonial "Pascataway." Beyond the obvious date of the 1630 Hilton patent, Jenness explained, Edward Hilton proved to be a "wise and prosperous merchant." He was, therefore, unlikely to make the "rash and foolhardy" decision to set up an isolated outpost in the heart of Indian territory in 1623.

"At that point, not a white man dwelt within all the borders of New Hampshire," Jenness wrote. Thompson was hours away by boat and Hilton's brother, William, was living in Massachusetts. Hubbard, "the careless historian made a gross error," Jenness concluded.

Jenness was fired up by a decision of the New Hampshire Legislature. The state planned to install a granite monument at Hilton's Point, certifying it, falsely, as a 1623 settlement. Yet "not a particle of contemporaneous testimony" had been found to support such a claim, Jenness argued. William Bradford, Edward Winslow, Christopher Levett, Phineas Pratt, and Samuel Maverick all visited Thompson at Little Harbor, not to mention documented visits by Miles Standish, Governor Robert Gorges, and merchant Thomas Weston. Not one man, it seems, having traveled 3,000 miles by sea, managed to cover the extra few miles to visit the only other Englishman in the region. No one mentioned Hilton, Jenness concluded, because he simply wasn't there.

Portsmouth lawyer Frank W. Hackett leapt into the continuing debate in 1886. While editing the city's earliest town records for publication, Hackett praised Jenness's and Deane's efforts to correct deep-rooted errors in New Hampshire history. The question whether Thompson—and not Hilton—had arrived in 1623 "ought surely to be treated as forever put to rest," Hackett wrote.

"There seems now to be no good reason for delaying the erection of a plain granite shaft at Odiorne's [sic] Point, to mark the site of the founding of New Hampshire," Hackett proclaimed.

It is unknown whether Edward Hilton ever set up expansive and expensive fishing flakes for drying fish. His patent suggests the outpost was primarily for trading and farming. Jenness reiterated that such an operation, established deep into Indian territory, was more than unlikely. Why travel miles to the mouth of the Piscataqua in a small boat only to head further out to the fishing grounds that were already in use by hundreds of seasonal fishers working on the Isles of Shoals and at Little Harbor? Returning the added distance to Hilton's Point against one of the strongest tides in the Americas, would only make the operation more difficult, time consuming, and dangerous, Jenness pointed out. The current at one spot on the river was so treacherous it became known locally as "Pull and Be Damned Point."

Despite overwhelming evidence to the contrary, a survey of New Hampshire history books and articles shows the Hilton claim is alive and well. But there has been progress. In his 862-page *History of New Hampshire (1888)*, John McClintock described the Dover claim as "absurd." An editor of *Granite Monthly* magazine, McClintock wrote: "It cannot be believed that Hilton founded a plantation at Hilton's Point in 1623, seven years before he got a deed of the land."

Perhaps, McClintock suggested, Edward Hilton was indeed one of the men sent out by Thompson's investors. As David's interest turned toward Boston, Edward Hilton may have taken the lead role at Little Harbor, while establishing a rudimentary seasonal trading post with the Indians at Dover Point. On learning of Thompson's death in 1627 or 1628, having no claim of his own, Edward may have returned to England to secure a patent. McClintock's scenario has merit.

By the 1880s, a Colonial Revival movement was in full swing. Faced with a fast-paced new Machine Age, Americans looked back with nostalgia to a seemingly simpler era. Arts, architecture, and historic preservation flourished, although a patriotic veneration for the spirit of the past often trumped accuracy. Amateur historians were increasingly drawn to reprinted works by Phineas Pratt, Christopher Levett, Sir Ferdinando Gorges, Samuel Maverick, and others—all confirming the Thompson story. By 1899, the Thompsons had their own plaque at Odiorne Point. It remains embedded into a tombstone-shaped rock sponsored by the National Society of Colonial Dames of America.

Individual town chronicles, usually produced by white Christian males, began to pop up across New Hampshire. In his 1905 *History of Rye*, Langdon Parsons naturally sided with the Thompsons. George Wadleigh, however, was in a quandary with his *Notable Events in the History of Dover, NH* (1913). It begins: "The first settlement of Dover, as well as of New Hampshire, is involved in some obscurity."

Wadleigh devoted much of his first chapter to wrestling with what he considered an effort by John Scribner Jenness to "discredit" Hubbard. Wadleigh conceded that "if a mere fishing and trading post" qualified, then Thompson was probably the first New Hampshire settler, even though he abandoned his site.

The Hilton brothers, too, were short-term residents of the spot that bears their name. Edward Hilton soon sold his Dover Point patent to Mr. Thomas Wiggin and moved to what is now the town of Newfields, once part of Exeter. Edward died there in 1671 at age seventy-six. Although he was not a Separatist, brother William Hilton and his wife received a grant of land to farm near New Plymouth. They had a third child there in 1624. It is not clear why William and his family were invited to leave the settlement for the Piscataqua. There was a disagreement between the Wiggins and the Pilgrims, quite possibly over the baptism of Hilton's child, since William Hilton was a "stranger" and not a Separatist. After Dover, William Hilton moved to Kittery and was sixty-six when he died at York, Maine, in 1656.

Their colony survived without them. Their settlement, briefly known as Wecohamet, was renamed Northam, and eventually became Dover. Once established, likely around 1628, Dover has a reasonable claim to the title "New Hampshire's first permanent settlement," edging out Strawberry Bank (1630) by two years. The Dover claim assumes no fishermen were left at Pannaway from 1628 (when someone contributed to William Bradford's fund to exile Thomas Morton) to 1630 (when Walter Neale and his team took possession of Little Harbor). Charles Knowles Bolton, a prolific history writer, suggested in 1929 that "men of ability were permanently settled" at both Hilton's Point and Little Harbor.

To be fair, we should call the battle for New Hampshire's first permanent European settlement a draw. It is, after all, a tempest in a teapot. Technically, the Piscataqua was still considered part of the territory of Maine at the time. "I know it is a bitter pill for any New Hampshire native to swallow," says a local scholar who prefers to remain anonymous, "but nothing really resembling New Hampshire existed until the Puritans from Massachusetts moved in."

George Wadleigh's 1913 book, published in Dover, showed progress in dealing responsibly with the Hilton legend. It was followed, however, with a 300th anniversary volume by John Scales, a local school principal and editor of the *Dover Daily Republican* and *Dover Enquirer*. His tercentenary souvenir history of the city was published by the Dover City Council in 1923. Scales doubled down on the Hilton legend, insisting that both brothers arrived on the ship *Providence of Plymouth* and immediately established their operation in 1623.

Scales devoted considerable ink to the life of David Thompson, but with a surprising twist. According to Scales, David made an unrecorded scouting trip to the region in 1622. He then set up a salmon fishing outpost at "Thompson Point," a spot on the map where the Piscataqua meets the Cochecho River in Dover. David then hurried back to England in time to collect his patent for Little Harbor. The theory appears to be pure fiction.

John Scales was no doubt referring to a July 1622 patent issued at London to David Thompson and a Mr. Jobe and Mr. Sherwood. It conditionally granted them rights to "a pt of Piscattowa River in New England." The cost and logistics of an expedition to the New World were daunting. Not all patents were acted upon, including one from the same year by Ferdinando Gorges and John Mason. It is implausible that Thompson could equip a voyage, sail to America, and return to England in time to receive his Little Harbor patent a few months later. Council records do not mention the earlier patent again. "It may refer to some earlier project of Thompson's, never perfected," scholar Charles Deane wrote. At best, Deane noted, it shows us Thompson had his eye on a Piscataqua landing site. Scales, however, took the patent as confirmation of a journey.

The former Dover newspaper editor and teacher also maintained that Thomas Roberts, perhaps an apprentice to Edward Hilton, arrived at Little Harbor to work for Thompson in 1623. There is no proof of Scales' claim. But Roberts did live in Northam (Dover) after the two Hiltons left. He became an early royal governor of the colony and his descendants occupied Roberts Farm for three centuries. According to family legend, a giant oak tree on the farm "was old when Columbus came on his voyage of discovery." It reportedly marked the spot where the Hiltons stepped ashore in 1623.

Scales further referenced a "Thompson Point House" on the town's early tax records as belonging to David Thompson. But alas, he noted, the corroborating document was lost. Critics wondered whether Thompson Point might, instead, be named for William Thompson, another early resident of Northam. Clinging to his elaborate fantasy, Scales said that was impossible.

Near the alleged Hilton landing site is Pomeroy Cove, possibly named for one of David Thompson's investors from Plymouth, England—or for someone else. Based on the name alone, Scales concluded that Leonard Pomeroy, a merchant and the mayor of Plymouth, England, must have visited the New Hampshire seacoast. Pomeroy not only provided the mystery ship that delivered the Hiltons and Thomas Roberts to Dover, according to Scales, but Pomeroy came along for the ride. By this reasoning, Abraham Lincoln must have visited Lincoln, Nebraska, and at least thirty other towns named in his honor throughout the United States.

In lieu of facts, Scales' theory is based on a mythical salmon fishing outpost, a lost town tax record, an old oak tree, a couple of placenames, and an unrecorded ship from England carrying four undocumented passengers. As further proof, Scales quoted the very passage from William Hubbard that had been disproven by the most erudite and honored researchers on the topic. Nevertheless, the legend stuck.

A ten-by-thirty-foot mural on the second floor of the Dover City Hall evokes a Thanksgiving-style scene of the city's founding days. Painted in the mid-1930s with federal funding, it shows colonists and Natives trading furs, fishing, and planting corn in harmony. Years later, a Dover high school French instructor named Mildred G. Flanders theorized that the Hilton brothers "used a great good more intelligence. . . than the Pilgrims." Instead of arriving at a random spot with no pioneer skills, Flanders told the local newspaper, the dauntless Dover settlers had tested the region before seeking a patent. The Hiltons, she claimed, worked their settlement unnoticed from 1623 to 1628. Convinced they had found the ideal spot, the Hiltons then sailed back to England to obtain a grant from the Council. Her fictional founding appeared in the 1949 book, *Land of the Free: A Pioneer Story for Children.*

These artistic projects and frequent anniversary celebrations reinforced the popular legend. Local historian Nelson Lawry recalled being asked in 1972 to join the committee planning a publication for Dover's 350th anniversary. His research, however, revealed the 1623 date was invalid. Lawry jokingly wrote:

> *I shared my reservations with the chair, who gave me a look*
> *somewhere between horror (would I upset the applecart?) and*
> *suspicion (was I an agent provocateur in the pay of Portsmouth?).*
> *Essentially, I was instructed to do the job I was assigned, keep my*
> *mouth shut, and get outta town, the sooner the better.*

Lawry went off to college. A quarter-century later, during the city's 375th event in 1998, he penned a piece for the *Dover Times.* "Despite all the hoopla and the stories in the local papers, including this one," he wrote, "ain't no way the place goes back that far." Town pride and tradition are powerful forces. When questioned for this book, local experts continued to cite Hubbard, Belknap, and Scales as confirmation of the Hilton claim. At this writing, the Dover city seal still reads "Town Settled 1623."

CHAPTER 25
The Laconia Company

Sir Ferdinando Gorges would not give up. From the failure of the 1607 Popham Colony in Maine, he had suffered one "wonderful discouragement" after another. Despite three fateful efforts by Captain John Smith, Levett's washout at Casco Bay, the Wessagusset double disaster, Morton's exile from Mare Mount, and other failures, Gorges was still determined to create a profitable kingdom in New England. News of David Thompson's death in 1628 was just another speed bump. Whatever his relationship with Thompson had been, Gorges would no longer mention the young apothecary.

Next on deck was Captain John Mason, whom Thompson had recommended in his 1625 letter. In the model of John Smith, Mason was an accomplished soldier, adventurer, cartographer, and entrepreneur. Like Smith, he had visited the New England coastline. If anyone was going to plant a profitable colony, it was him. And yet, while often called "The Father of New Hampshire," John Mason is little more than a ghostly smudge in most histories of the state.

Born in Norfolk, well educated, young Mason was already a successful sea captain with his own ship in trade with Amsterdam. But frustrated by business deals gone wrong, he turned to piracy, capturing merchant ships in the waters between Scotland and Norway. Mason owned a small island reputed to be a way-station for pirates and thieves. He was arrested, stripped of his ship and all his goods, and thrown into an Edinburgh prison in 1615—details mysteriously missing from most New Hampshire history texts.

Through the influence of Scottish friends, Mason earned a new and dangerous position as governor of a fishing outpost in Newfoundland. His successful six-year term there gave him the opportunity to explore the North Atlantic coast. Back in England by 1621, Mason partnered with Sir Ferdinando in a shared quest to build a settlement. "In John Mason," according to Maine historian James Phinney Baxter, Gorges "had found a promising helper, a man of sound judgment and full of energy."

The two men received a patent in 1622 for land stretching from the Merrimack River in modern Newburyport, Massachusetts, to the Kennebec River at Bath, Maine. But unable to find willing investors, they could not launch a colony. This unused grant would later confuse New Hampshire historians.

Mason returned to military duty. In 1627, as the Thompsons were starting over in Boston Bay, John Mason bought a house, then known as the Greyhound Tavern in Portsmouth, England. A year later, the powerful Sir George Villiers, best known as the Duke of Buckingham, attended an event at Mason's home. Although a favorite of King Charles I, Villiers was a lightning rod for trouble. He had arranged the king's controversial marriage to a Roman Catholic wife. Worse, Villiers had organized disastrous naval conflicts against both Spain and France. Coincidentally, he was also a member of the Council for New England.

In 1628, Villiers was stabbed to death at John Mason's home. That incident, too, rarely appears in New Hampshire history books. The site of the assassination is now a guest house known as "Ye Spotted Dogge." In a detailed study of the famous murder, while describing Captain Mason, an English scholar wrote, "His busy brain was always hatching schemes for getting rich and nothing was too far fetched."

With Thompson's Little Harbor experiment now doomed, Mason

and Gorges teamed up again. But English politics had shifted wildly in the seven years since their first partnership. King James I, a supporter of the Council for New England, was dead. Charles I, his successor, was in a perpetual power struggle with a Parliament that disapproved of both the king's marriage and his loyalty to the late Duke of Buckingham. Tired of being told what to do, Charles I decided to run the country on his own. In March of 1629, the king dismissed Parliament. He did not order Parliament members back into session until 1640.

Strawberry Bank was born during this period known to opponents of the monarchy as "The Eleven Years Tyranny." Royalists like Gorges and Mason would likely prefer the alternate title, "The Era of Personal Rule." While King Charles had the legal right to shutter Parliament, there was a big problem. Funds to run the government continued to flow in from feudal dues, from the king's personal estates, and from custom duties. But it wasn't enough. In the event of a future war—and war was always on the horizon—he needed permission from Parliament to authorize a general tax.

So, money was tight in the 1630s. To pick up the slack, King Charles and his advisers developed a series of funding schemes. They added ship fees on coastal towns, sold off royal lands, and granted monopolies. The Council for New England's effort to dominate the Atlantic fishing industry, mentioned earlier, was among these unpopular monopolies. Meanwhile, Puritan power was on the rise in England even as thousands of Puritans were moving to Massachusetts. For men loyal to the Crown, like Mason and Gorges, time to establish profitable Anglican colonies in New England was running out.

To understand why Mason set up his colony at Strawberry Bank at this moment in history, a little background is required. French exploration of North America, we should remember, was well underway by the mid-1500s. Unlike most English traders, the French developed a strong relationship of mutual gain with the indigenous people living there. Their booming fur trade was centered at Lake Champlain, nestled between the northern borders of New York and Vermont.

During one of many wars with France, the Anglo-French War (1627 to 1629), a large group of London merchants saw a chance to use the conflict to tap into the fur market. They created the Company of Adventurers to Canada. Sanctioned for privateering by King Charles, they hoped to overpower the French along the St. Lawrence River and to take control of the fur business at Lake Champlain.

In 1629, the English privateers forced the surrender of the New France stronghold at Quebec City on the St. Lawrence. Samuel de Champlain, the famous explorer, was delivered to London among French prisoners of war. The victorious Company of Adventurers then applied to the king for sole rights to trade in the newly conquered area of New France. The conquest, however, came too late. A treaty had already been signed and, since privateering was only legal during war, the captured region was given back to the French.

Were Mason and Gorges, both veteran soldiers, involved in the effort to take over the French fur trade? Historians Charles Deane and John Scribner Jenness suggested exactly that. In 1629, learning of the fall of New France, Mason and Gorges and a group of investors quickly formed the Laconia Company. Their 1629 indenture from the Council allowed "the planting, ruling, and governing" of a vague place to be called "Laconia."

This unspecified spot was located somewhere near "the lakes and rivers of the Iroquois" inhabited by "nations of savage people." Laconia, according to the 1629 indenture, "falls into the river of Canada." Was the name "Laconia," derived from a region in Greece, as is often proposed? Or was it simply a made-up classical-sounding word (Lake-onia) following a popular pattern of the times? York, Maine, for instance, was once called "Gorgeana" in honor of Ferdinando Gorges.

With the St. Lawrence back in French hands, Laconia Company

investors were banking on a popular theory that the deep fast-flowing Piscataqua River was an alternate route to the fur trading center at Lake Champlain. Based on 1629 data, this made sense. Europeans had long been searching for a water passage through the American continent to the Pacific. An alternate route to Lake Champlain, estimated to be about 100 miles inland, seemed more than likely. Native legends confirmed the existence of a great lake within a few days' journey from the "Crystal Hills" (White Mountains) that were rich with glittering metal and gems.

Thomas Morton, who also believed in the legend of the lakes, may have encouraged Mason and Gorges to search them out. David Thompson also considered going there. "Neither is it far in likelihood from the place I dwell in," Thompson wrote in 1625, "over to the river of Canada, for the great lake which is in the French maps called 'Lac de Champlain' is but a day and a half journey from my house. I intend, God willing, to see it in a month hence."

"The scheme of these patentees is apparent from the grant itself," Jenness wrote of Gorges and Mason's plan. The thousand-acre Strawberry Bank settlement, Jenness realized, was to be a commercial way-station. Trade goods from Europe would be stockpiled at the landing site, now Portsmouth's Prescott Park area, about three miles from the mouth of the Piscataqua River. English traders in boats or canoes would continue the journey upriver to barter with the Natives at Lake Champlain. Returning down the Piscataqua with the valuable pelts, they would export them back to Europe.

"Fabulous stories had reached England of the vast wealth of this region in furs, and the prospect of a lucrative trade with the inhabitants of the lake country was attractive," Maine historian James Phinney Baxter wrote. The English called their destination the Lake of the Iroquois, Baxter suggested, because they were reluctant to credit the "discovery" to French explorer Samuel de Champlain.

The true origin of Strawberry Bank as a transit point for Indian trade has been downplayed if not entirely ignored by most modern historians. But it was well known at the time. Even the incoming Massachusetts governor, John Winthrop, knew what Mason and Gorges were up to. In his journal, Winthrop mentioned Mason's attempted "discovery of the Lake of New England." William Hubbard, in his early history of New England, referred to Laconia as John Mason's quest to find "an imaginary province."

It didn't take long for Mason's advance team under Captain Walter Neale to learn the shiny stuff at the Crystal Hills was mica and garnets, two worthless minerals. Instead of the legendary Northwest Passage to the fabled "Laconia," the great body of water the Natives saw from the White Mountains was probably Lake Winnipesaukee. Laconia Company investors waited, impatiently, to strike it rich. But even greater disappointment lay ahead.

CHAPTER 26
About Strawberry Bank

It is easy to confuse John Mason's 1630 Piscataqua "plantation" known as Strawberry Bank (later Portsmouth) with Strawbery Banke Museum located today on the city's waterfront. The ten-acre museum probably includes the spot where the original "Great House" sheltered the settlers who lived communally while struggling to turn a profit for the Laconia Company back in England. Remnants of New Hampshire's second European-built home were reportedly still standing in 1690. Artifacts may yet lie beneath the soil near the raised garden beds off Marcy Street across from Prescott Park. But there the seventeenth-century connection ends.

The secluded tidal inlet known as Puddle Dock that attracted the Strawberry Bankers was once large enough for small boats. But the salty creek clogged up over time. It became a garbage dump and was filled in more than a century ago, creating a flat central activity area at Strawbery Banke Museum. The Sherburne House, with its two distinctive gables, built between 1695 and 1705, is the only visible link between the nonprofit museum and the seventeenth century.

In 1630, John Mason sent Captain Walter Neale and a small company of soldiers to establish a base of operations on the Piscataqua. Before selecting the Puddle Dock site, they moved into the former Thompson house at Little Harbor. With David dead and Amias settled in Boston, the Council for New England apparently did not recognize any previous ownership of the Pannaway property. Thompson had also not fulfilled the five-year indenture contract with his investors.

Whether Pannaway had been abandoned, as some historians suggest, or was still occupied, is unclear. Nathaniel Adams, writing in 1825, suggested Captain Neale took over a working business that included six great shallops, five fishing boats with sails, anchors, cables, and thirteen skiffs. But this list comes from a 1635 inventory of Strawberry Bank, five years later. Referencing Neale's brief stay at Little Harbor, Maine historian James Phinney Baxter referred to Pannaway as the "Governor's House." From the Council's perspective, Walter Neale was the region's third governor following the deaths of Robert Gorges and David Thompson.

Another patent issued to Ferdinando Gorges and Mason in the summer of 1631 conferred the Pannaway title to the Laconia Company, including a "house and chief habitation... wherein Captain Walter Neale and the company with him now doth or lately did reside, together with the gardens and corn ground occupied and planted by the said colony and the salt works already begun."

Having taken over Little Harbor, the Laconia Company also expanded the Strawberry Bank claim. It came to include the towns of Rye, Greenland, New Castle, Portsmouth, Newington, the Isles of Shoals, and Salmon Falls (South Berwick, Maine). This document also split the holdings of the two patentees right up the middle of the Piscataqua River from Salmon Falls to the Isles of Shoals. Gorges took Maine and Mason took New Hampshire, although both men remained in England.

If the Thompsons and Hiltons were the first British citizens to inhabit New Hampshire, Walter Neale and his anonymous crew were next. Lacking any physical description, we can safely imagine Neale as a less irascible armor-plated version of Miles Standish. Like Gorges, Smith, and Mason, he had been a soldier. Before acting as Mason's paid police chief and governor, Neale wrote that he "hath never had any other profession but his sword, nor any fortunes than the war."

A staunch Anglican like his employers, Neale quickly ran up against Thomas Wiggin, reputed to be a Puritan soldier. Wiggin, by some accounts, had been sent from Salem to occupy Edward Hilton's new colony at Dover Point. The Strawberry Bank and Hilton grants clearly overlapped. The two military leaders met, legend says, with their tiny armies at "Bloody Point" in what is now the town of Newington. The nickname may be ironic, since Neale and Wiggin agreed to split up the Piscataqua territory peacefully. No blood was spilled at Bloody Point.

Portsmouth historian Bruce Ingmire has suggested this "non-battle" helped define the character of the region at a very early point in its history. Strawberry Bank was not going to be like the Massachusetts Bay Colony. It would be tolerant and nonconformist, guided more by the will of an independent people than by its intolerant Puritan neighbors.

By 1631, Neale was in charge of eighty stewards, agents, artisans, women, and indentured servants who arrived aboard the ships *Pied Cow* and *Warwick*. When danger threatened the Great House at Puddle Dock, Neale and a flotilla of six small boats headed north in pursuit of the English pirate Dixie Bull, but they saw no trace of him. Finding the fabled Lake of the Iroquois, meanwhile, was his prime objective. When his first quest failed, Neale turned to Plan B.

"A desire to discover gold pervaded the minds of the colonists," Edwin A. Carleton wrote in *New Hampshire As It Is* (1855). "New Hampshire being a mountainous region, was deemed likely to abound in the precious metals." In 1632, Neale led a small team toward the White Mountains of New Hampshire. Thomas Gorges, a nephew of Sir Ferdinando, later reported the group was forced to turn back when they ran out of food. The heavy "crystal stones" they collected, as mentioned earlier, proved to be worthless.

Other prospecting trips yielded nothing of value. Neale returned to England empty-handed. As reported in the *Provincial Papers,* a frustrated John Mason wrote to one of his agents at Strawberry Bank on May 5, 1634. "I have disbursed a great deal of money in the plantation and never received one penny," Mason wrote, "but hope if there was once a discovery of the Lakes, that I should, in some reasonable time, be reimbursed again."

Ambrose Gibbons, Mason's agent at Strawberry Bank, wrote back. "I perceive you have a great mind for the Lakes, and I as great a will to assist you. If I had 2 horses and 3 men with me, I would by God's help soon resolve you of the situation of it, if not to live there myself."

Early correspondence between Mason and his colonial agents followed a similar pattern. The colonists desperately needed things from England. Settlers begged for fish hooks and lines, nails, spikes, locks, hinges, beds, leather, rugs, more men, wives, seed, malt for beer, farm logging tools, shoes, Indian trade goods, blankets, and clothes. Mason's investors wanted results. Their language is polite, but insistent. "We hope you will find out some good mines," investor Tom Eyre wrote from England, "which will be welcome news unto us."

But there would be no quick profits. Despite being given a sixteenth-century book (written in Latin) on how to find and process precious metals, the settlers found no mines. Efforts to transplant grape vines for making wine were also unsuccessful. Despite some good fur trading by sawmill owner Humphrey Chadbourne at the Salmon Falls post, the Laconia Company began holding back on supplies and requiring payment on demand in beaver pelts. Ambrose Gibbons, writing from Strawberry Bank in 1633, reminded his investors that a plantation could not be built on words. "Those that have been here this three years," Gibbons wrote of his fellow settlers, "some of them have neither meat, money, nor clothes—a great disparagement."

Mason's short-lived Piscataqua experiment from 1630 to 1635 coincides precisely with the first wave of the Great Migration to

Massachusetts. Puritan culture is so ingrained in our view of New England it is difficult to believe it might have failed. It was during this period, back in England, that lawyer Thomas Morton was working with Mason and Gorges to revoke the Pilgrim and Puritan charters to Massachusetts. The three Anglicans, according to Puritan historian John Abbott Goodwin, were "malignant enemies" of New Plymouth and the Massachusetts Bay Colony. John Winthrop complained that Mason and his cohorts were petitioning the Privy Council with "many false accusations" against the Puritans.

Mason was now at the peak of his power. He was a leading member of the Council and had been appointed Vice Admiral of New England. Instead of a Puritan theocracy, Mason and Gorges imagined themselves as proprietary landholders. Their plan, as proposed to King Charles, would have boosted the English economy, solved the nation's overpopulation and poverty problems, provided endless timber for the creation of a maritime empire, spread the Anglican faith to the indigenous people, and prevented the French and Spanish from swallowing the rest of the North American continent. In return for all this, Mason and Gorges wanted to rule New England like kings—assigning land grants, charging rent, collecting taxes, writing laws, and disbursing justice.

"This was a very great design," Mason's biographer Charles Ward Tuttle wrote, "and had it been carried out, who can say what would have been the history of New England today?" Mason's advantage, however, quickly eroded.

Governor Winthrop wrote: "But through the Lord's good providence, and the care of our friends in England. . . and the good testimony given on our behalf by one Captain Wiggin (who dwelt at Pascataqua and had been diverse times among us) their malicious practice took not effect." Thomas Wiggin, the leader of what would become Dover, therefore, played a pivotal role in preventing the Council from driving the Puritans out of Massachusetts.

In the spring of 1634, according to Tuttle, Mason sent his agent Henry Josselyn and more men to build a sawmill and gristmill at Newichawanock, on what is now the Great Works River in South Berwick, Maine. In 1635, he received title to an additional 10,000 acres to the west of the Kennebec River. Preparing to come to the rescue of his Strawberry Bank colonists, Captain John Mason filled a ship with provisions in England. He was about to board the vessel for a triumphant trip to New Hampshire. Before he could depart, Mason grew ill and died suddenly in December 1635. The ship never sailed.

And that was it. The Council for New England disbanded. The Laconia Company investors pulled out. When the stranded Piscataqua settlers begged widow Anne Mason to keep her husband's venture alive, she rejected them outright. She then instructed Ambrose Gibbons to sell the swine in his Strawberry Bank stable to pay her lawyer's fees.

More letters went unanswered. Stockpiles dwindled. As one harsh New England winter bled into the next, the men and women of Strawberry Bank woke up to reality. The Lake of the Iroquois was a pipe dream. There were no gold mines. Their leader was dead. Deep in the heart of darkness, 3,000 miles from home—they were on their own.

CHAPTER 27
Our Crazy Granite State Start-Up

A sk any New Hampshire resident how the Granite State began. With luck, you may hear tales of Dawnland tribes, seasonal European fishers, Piscataqua settlements, or lumber and sawmills. More likely the question prompts images of cartoon Pilgrims followed by a sudden leap to the Revolutionary War, the defunct Old Man of the Mountain, and a debate over the meaning of "Live Free or Die." In schools, New Hampshire history is relegated to the fourth grade where students hop from Native culture to revolutionary John Stark, President Franklin Pierce, and on to the Civil War. David Thompson occasionally makes a cameo appearance, often linked without evidence to the Hilton brothers. He is inevitably depicted as a fisherman, rarely as an apothecary, and almost never as the deputy governor of all New England. Amias Thompson Maverick, who survived into her seventies, is among the missing.

Early New Hampshire history is confusing, but it is not unknowable. An inventory of English goods at Pascataway (Strawberry Bank) recorded in July 1635, for example, offers a snapshot of pioneer life. The document lists a significant cache of weapons, a single Bible, a guide to mining for precious metals, and limited food stores. The list also catalogs items of clothing, building materials, tools, fishing gear, cooking utensils, bolts of cloth and canvas, and more.

The list of precious livestock alone paints a crisp picture of communal life at the Great House at Puddle Dock. There were "31 cows (cattle), 3 bulls, 15 steers and heifers, 12 calves, 63 sheep, 29 lambs, 52 goats, 67 hogs (old and young), 19 mares, horses and colts." The inventory also contains the names of all male servants and stewards, but identifies none of the women.

The Puritans interpreted the death of John Mason in 1635, as they interpreted everything—one more step in a divine master plan to plant their Christian "city on a hill" in America. "But the Lord in mercy, taking him [Mason] away, all the business fell on sleep," John Winthrop wrote. The Council's effort to monopolize the fishing industry and Indian trade also collapsed.

Sir Ferdinando Gorges was appointed governor of New England in 1637. Two years later, he was granted a patent for the territory of Maine. There was talk of sending 1,000 soldiers across the sea to enforce royal laws and Church of England practices on the expanding Puritan settlements. But no funds to raise, equip, and transport such a private force were available.

When a supply ship built by Gorges fell to pieces at the dock, Winthrop was doubly certain that the Almighty was on his side. Now seventy years old, his health and wealth fading, Gorges could not endure a passage to New England. He died in 1647, forty years after the initial failure of the Popham Colony. Thirty years later, his grandson, another Ferdinando Gorges, sold all rights to Maine to Massachusetts for £1,250. Maine would not become an independent state until 1820.

The early history of New Hampshire, meanwhile, is a hash of politics and property disputes. The confusion comes from three warring factions—the Mason family, the succession of English leaders, and Massachusetts Bay.

Captain John Mason and his wife Anne had only one child. Their daughter, also named Anne, married John Tufton of Sussex. She bore three sons and two daughters. Captain Mason bequeathed his perceived land grants—including about twenty miles of New Hampshire coastline—to his eldest grandson, John, on the condition he change his last name to Mason. John Tufton Mason obligingly changed his name, but died childless. John's inherited real estate passed to his brother Robert, who also assumed the Mason name. Already, we can see how complex the Masonian claim to New Hampshire becomes.

Robert Tufton Mason imagined a potential windfall collecting annual land rental fees from property owners in the expanding province. He tried every tactic from litigation to intimidation, but with minimal success. At Robert's death in 1688, the Piscataqua claim passed to his sons, Robert and John. But in the words of an early historian, Robert's sons were unwilling to "assume the burden of their father's unprofitable attempts to evict angry settlers and recover the estate by the tedious and expensive process of law." Instead, they cashed out.

In 1691, Captain Mason's great-grandchildren sold what by this time amounted to the entire province for £750, equal to $200,000 today. New Hampshire was sold and resold to a series of wealthy "Masonian Proprietors." As the battle for ownership continued, the province grew inland, town by town, adding another two million acres to the supposed Mason grant. (For the record, Mason died before his New Hampshire grant was officially approved, leading some scholars to conclude his family never owned anything.) The witheringly dull legal battles continued well beyond the American Revolution.

The second source of our confusing past is tied to the violent shifts in English politics. Captain Mason and the Laconia Company were Anglican agents of King Charles I. But in 1649, having been convicted of treason under Oliver Cromwell's Puritan leadership, the king was beheaded in a public execution. Cromwell's reign, however, was short-lived, and he died in 1658. King Charles II, son of Charles I, restored the monarchy two years later. Cromwell's corpse was exhumed, put through a mock trial for treason, and hanged. His severed head was displayed on a pole outside Westminster Hall. These seismic reversals of power in Britain directly impacted the already rocky governing of New Hampshire.

As a succession of distant English leaders tried to rule its American possessions through local governors, the Massachusetts Bay Colony tried to assimilate the Piscataqua territory and beyond. These tangled boundaries added a third level of confusion to the New Hampshire story.

In 1641, the seacoast region was a patchwork of four, raw self-governing settlements. But life in the wilderness was scary. Dover, Exeter, and Hampton, largely managed by local Puritans, agreed to be taken under the protective wing of Massachusetts. At first, Strawberry Bankers resisted Puritan domination. Having settled without authority onto property abandoned by the Laconia Company, they held their ground. More than the threat from pirates, Indians, the French, the Spanish, the bitter cold, wild animals, disease, starvation, or Puritan laws—the orphaned settlers of Captain Mason's colony feared losing their land.

But resistance was futile and the Piscataqua region soon fell under Massachusetts control. Upon reclaiming the throne, Charles II was unhappy with the Puritans running New England. No surprise there. In 1679, the "Merry Monarch" declared New Hampshire to be a Crown Colony, subject to the laws of the Church of England. In doing so, the king drove a royal wedge between Puritan-dominated Massachusetts and the Puritan-dominated territory of Maine, forever changing the course of Granite State history. Beginning in the mid-1700s, a dynasty of wealthy royal governors, all named Wentworth and living in Portsmouth, would shake off Massachusetts' authority. But New Hampshire ties to the Bay State run deep.

VI. CELEBRATION

"I call it an old town, but it is only relatively old. When one reflects on the countless centuries that have gone to the formation of this crust of earth on which we temporarily move, the most ancient cities on its surface seem merely things of the week before last."

—*Thomas Bailey Aldrich*, An Old Town by the Sea, *1883*

"Hitherto, our Colonial history has received less attention than it has deserved."

— *Joseph B. Walker at the 1899 dedication of a monument at Odiorne Point*

"Of all the New Hampshire towns, Portsmouth is the most glamorous and romantic."

— *Ella Shannon Bowles*, Let Me Show You New Hampshire, *1938*

CHAPTER 28
Worshiping the Pilgrims

In July 1623, as David Thompson was delivering a lifesaving load of fish to the Pilgrims, more settlers arrived at New Plymouth. The supply ship *Anne* and the pinnace *Little James* were sponsored by the controversial Thomas Weston and his Merchant Adventurers. Among the ninety-odd passengers were future wives of Governor William Bradford and Wessagusset survivor Phineas Pratt. Another passenger, fifteen-year-old John Faunce, would unknowingly launch one of the most enduring legends in American history.

John and his wife Patience Faunce had eight children. Thomas Faunce, born in 1647, was only seven years old when his father died. It wasn't until 1741, when Thomas was ninety-four and a church elder, that he identified a granite boulder in Plymouth Harbor as the 1620 landing site of the *Mayflower*. Witnesses later reported that Thomas Faunce claimed to have heard the story from his father, who had heard it from the original settlers.

"Whether Faunce's assertion was accurate oral history," Christopher Klein wrote for *History.com*, "or the figment of a doddering old mind, we don't know." In 1774, townspeople tried to remove and preserve Plymouth Rock using twenty yoke of oxen. The ten-ton boulder cracked in half. One chunk was dragged to the Plymouth town square, where it became a symbol of liberty for rowdy revolutionaries.

At first, venerating the self-appointed saints of New Plymouth was a local thing. In 1789 the Old Colony Club, an exclusive men's society, created Forefather's Day, an annual celebration still observed in Plymouth. Senator (later president) John Quincy Adams spoke at Forefather's Day in 1802. The Pilgrim Society, incorporated in 1820, then established "America's oldest continuously operating public museum."

On December 22, 1820, Daniel Webster gave a stirring speech in Plymouth. The famed orator had cut his teeth as a young lawyer in Portsmouth, New Hampshire, but was then living in Boston. His keynote address at the bicentennial of the *Mayflower* landing was widely reprinted and greatly enhanced his notoriety. In his speech, Webster laid the foundations for what is currently known as heritage tourism. Historic sites, he said, draw visitors with a special power and purpose. Gesturing toward the legendary Plymouth Rock, Webster called upon the "genius of the place which inspires and awes us." He continued:

> *We feel that we are on the spot where the first scene of our history was laid; where the hearths and altars of New England were first placed; where Christianity, and civilization, and letters made their first lodgement, in a vast extent of country, covered with a wilderness, and peopled by roving barbarians.*

Again, thousands of years of indigenous occupants were cast aside. And like so many Puritan historians to follow, Webster promoted a theory that the Pilgrims were agents of a divine plan. Christianity and "civilization" were synonyms. Like the Puritans who followed, the Pilgrims were credited with bringing order, light, and faith to what they saw as a chaotic, dark, and godless continent. This religious zealotry merged easily with the new nation's patriotic spirit following the War of 1812.

The speeches, toasts, and parades surrounding the Second Centennial celebration at Plymouth in 1820 were commercial and political, too. The rediscovery of the largely forgotten Separatists of New Plymouth was part of an organized effort to draw attention back to New England and away from Virginia, Philadelphia, New York, and other historic locations. No one could dispute the 1607 settlement at Jamestown or the 1776 signing of the Declaration of Independence at the Pennsylvania State House. But Massachusetts could, at least, grab the moral high ground—as long as one ignored its early treatment of Natives, Africans, and everyone who didn't ascribe to strict Puritan teachings.

The movement to establish New England as the rightful "birthplace" of America grew up largely among elite Harvard graduates, Congregational ministers, and Unitarian intellectuals. Jamestown might have seniority, they reasoned, but no southern or western location could hold a candle to the purifying intentions of the Pilgrim fathers and mothers. Through the fog of two centuries, one small Separatist band of white English immigrants came to embody the fundamental characteristics of the ideal American. Their thrilling and well-documented story, picked clean of its unsavory elements, would become the basis of a national holiday. And nothing implied permanence and stability more than a smooth welcoming chunk of granite.

Plymouth Rock was moved to the hallowed Pilgrim Hall Museum in 1834. It was borne in a two-wheeled cart and accompanied by a marching band and a model of the *Mayflower*. But the rock fell off the cart and split in half again. Pieces went into the pockets of souvenir hunters, into churches, museums, and private collections. Half of the half of Plymouth Rock was housed in Pilgrim Hall. The other quarter, held together with mortar, went on public display, enshrined inside an iron fence beneath an ornate Tuscan-style stone canopy. In 1880, the quarried lower portion was crudely married to the upper part and the date "1620" etched in the rock. Rain fell, ice formed, vandals chiseled, and the mortar failed.

A century after Daniel Webster turned a rock into a tourist mecca, the surviving pieces were re-assembled and waterproofed. The Victorian-era portico was replaced by a larger Neo-Classical Revival-style shrine. According to *New Yorker* writer John McPhee, fragments of Plymouth Rock have been turned into paperweights, tie tacks, pendants, earrings, and cufflinks. Its flat potato-shape has been reproduced into everything from coin banks to Jello molds. McPhee sent thin shards of the rock for analysis by experts. The glacial pebble, he was told, was formed 680 million years ago—give or take seventeen million years—in the primeval continent of Atlantica.

Meanwhile, thanks in part to Daniel Webster, the Pilgrims were making a nineteenth-century comeback. Boston, once the birthplace of Puritan power, was becoming the literary hub of the nation and a press agent for its devout founders. Prior to the Civil War, New England writers like Nathaniel Hawthorne (*The Scarlet Letter*, 1850) and poet Henry Wadsworth Longfellow (*The Courtship of Miles Standish*, 1858) were fascinated by the colonial era. Both authors, it is worth mentioning, were encouraged and published by James T. Fields, the Portsmouth-born owner of the Boston book firm Ticknor & Fields.

In Longfellow's fictional romance, Miles Standish is driven to murder the Natives at Wessagusset because they taunted and insulted him. "The hot blood of his race. . . boiled and beat in his heart, and swelled in the veins of his temples," Longfellow wrote. The poem continues:

> *Headlong he leaped on the [Indian] boaster, and, snatching his knife*
> > *from its scabbard,*
> *Plunged it into his heart, and, reeling backward, the savage*
> *Fell with his face to the sky, and a fiendlike fierceness upon it.*

Victorian editions of the lengthy poem include an illustration of Miles Standish marching to New Plymouth with the head of his enemy impaled on a lance. The depiction of Standish as a righteous enforcer and a sympathetic figure, rather than a cutthroat, was essential to promoting the Pilgrim legend. A silent film version of *The Courtship of Miles Standish* appeared on the big screen in 1923. Created at a cost equivalent to over $50 million today, it was a box office flop, bankrupting its production company.

In 1856, as Longfellow was working on his epic poem, William Bradford's *Of Plymouth Plantation* appeared in print for the first time. Among the nascent nation's earliest literary works, it is considered an American classic, although it is too often taken as pure history. Frequently quoted, rarely read, Bradford's narrative can be shockingly candid. In 1636, for example, a list of capital offenses was drawn up by Pilgrim leaders. They included arson, murder, rape, sodomy, witchcraft, adultery, treason, and buggery or bestiality. Six years later, in 1642, a teenager named Thomas Granger was convicted of buggery. Following Old Testament law, Bradford reported, young Granger was put to death. But first, he was forced to watch all the animals with which he had carnal relations slaughtered before his eyes.

Samuel Eliot Morison edited a later edition of Bradford's journal. He wondered why the smaller and weaker Separatist colony so often overshadowed the early settlers of Virginia, South Carolina, and Massachusetts Bay. "Why are the Pilgrim Fathers and the Plymouth Colony so popular," Morison asked in 1954, "as to drive other colonial pioneers and founders out of the public mind?" First, Morison answered himself, was the quality and quantity of writing by Bradford and Edward Winslow. Second, of course, was Thanksgiving.

The backstory of our beloved holiday is well known. New Hampshire-born Sarah Josepha Hale peppered five American presidents with requests to make Thanksgiving a national holiday. There had been "Days of Public Thanksgiving" since George Washington in 1789, but it took Abraham Lincoln, amid the horror of the Civil War, to seal the deal. Books and magazine articles about the *Mayflower* targeted to children became ubiquitous in the Victorian era. The myth of a morally, intellectually, and technically superior race bonding with helpful and passive Natives was repeated annually in countless stories, greeting cards, books, magazine articles, pictures, church services, and school plays.

In an age brimming with memorials to the American Revolution and Civil War, the Pilgrims did surprisingly well. Visitors to Duxbury, Massachusetts, are still invited, in season, to climb 125 granite steps inside the Miles Standish Monument. Perched 200-feet above sea level, the 116-foot shaft is topped by a fourteen-foot tall statue of the Pilgrims' irascible military leader. Built in 1872, the statue was struck by lightning in 1922 when its head and arm blew off. The statue was repaired in 1930.

There is also a Miles Standish State Forest and campsite in Carver, Massachusetts, and a memorial stone cairn at Squaw Rock Park in Quincy. What may be the mortal remains of Captain Standish have been exhumed three times at the Old Burying Ground in Duxbury, which is ringed by four cannons aimed at tourists approaching from every direction.

In 1910, the 252-foot granite Pilgrim Monument opened atop High Pole Hill in Provincetown on Cape Cod. It marks the first landing site of the *Mayflower*. Changing with the times, a recent exhibition at the companion Provincetown Museum was entitled, "Our Story: The Complicated Relationship of the Indigenous Wampanoag and the Mayflower Pilgrims." Founded in 1947, the living museum known as Plimoth Plantation continues to tell and retell the Pilgrim story in a replica village where it is permanently 1627. Millions of tourists from around the globe have visited, drinking in the sights, smells, and sounds of life in the seventeenth century, in a year when David Thompson was still alive.

No such fame for Sir Ferdinando. The would-be-founder of New England is memorialized at Fort Gorges in Maine, a Civil War-era military base where no battles were fought and no troops were stationed. The ruins, located on Hog Island in Casco Bay, are owned by the city of Portland and accessible only by private boat tours. The old fort stands, according to *MaineBoats.com*, "as a curious landmark—isolated, proud, and largely forgotten, just like its namesake."

Following the 1953 release of *Gorges of Plymouth Fort*, a rare biography by Canadian historian Richard Arthur Preston, one scholarly reviewer summed things up. "Yet Ferdinando Gorges is almost unknown today, neglected except for a line or two in the textbooks—because he was unsuccessful. He lacked funds at crucial moments. He never came to America himself because he had not the cash to outfit an expedition—and he tangled with the Puritans, which accounts in part for the shabby treatment he has received from historians."

"In his own time," University of Bristol Dean, C. M. MacInnes said of Gorges, "he was looked upon as a failure and the historians of later centuries have tended to dismiss him as a reactionary bungler. It has often been suggested that his zeal for the glory of England was a mere mask to cover his selfish intentions. Such a view is both unfair and untrue." Unfair and shabby treatment, David Thompson might say, is better than none at all.

CHAPTER 29
A Bicentennial Bash

Portsmouth's maritime economy was booming when George Washington passed through in 1789, but it didn't last. By 1820, following three devastating downtown fires, Thomas Jefferson's crippling trade embargo, and the War of 1812, the once-thriving seaport was in decline. Its storied past was looking better than its uncertain future. With Pilgrim popularity making a comeback in Massachusetts and with the city's own bicentennial on the horizon, Portsmouth took a page from the Plymouth playbook. It was time to celebrate.

Unable to rival the *Mayflower* drama, Portsmouth leaders adopted a "merchant-adventurer" brand. In a speech delivered on May 21, 1823, newspaper publisher Nathaniel Haven, Jr. laid it on the line. Portsmouth, he said, did not begin with Pilgrims "seeking asylum for their persecuted church." Piscataqua settlers, instead, wanted to make money and own land. Our founders, Haven told his listeners, were endowed with a "commercial spirit" that transformed "a wild and tangled thicket" into a thriving seaport.

Haven's audience packed into ninety pews in the dilapidated North Church. More than a century old, the wooden structure had somehow survived the three downtown fires (1802, 1806, and 1813) that had turned hundreds of buildings into charred rubble.

"Our ancestors were of humbler rank," Haven said of Portsmouth's founders. They were men to be honored, but not idolized. Many were

Puritans, but religious freedom was not high on the to-do list of our "Piscataqua Planters."

Between the lines, New Hampshire, if not all of northern New England, was coming to accept its status as subservient to Massachusetts. The attempted "Puritan conquest" of the region, as historian Charles E. Clark called it, had left its mark. Massachusetts Bay laws shaped New Hampshire towns. Harvard-trained missionaries spread the gospel to the heathen fishermen at the Isles of Shoals. Boston, by Nathaniel Haven's era, was not only the hub of maritime commerce and the "Birthplace of the American Revolution," but the self-appointed moral and intellectual capital of the nation.

Portsmouth's hastily planned copycat anniversary was a badly needed ego boost for the town. Timed to match the spring arrival of David Thompson and his band of fishermen, the 1823 celebration drew many of the state's top politicians and intellectuals, including Daniel Webster.

Festivities began early, with an enormous formal procession. "Heaven seemed to smile propitiously on the occasion; for the weather was delightful," a local newspaper reported. The parade passed through the principal roads of the town. The route included the expanding elite neighborhoods along Middle and Pleasant streets. It advanced into the commercial Market Street, down through the evolving North End, and back into the central Parade, now Market Square. Conspicuously absent from the parade route was the fading waterfront area of Puddle Dock.

Dressed in full regalia, members of the fraternal society of Freemasons marched to beating drums, escorted by two light-infantry companies. Then came the Merchant's Association, followed by members of the clergy, military officers, prominent citizens, and schoolmasters herding their young scholars forward. At the North Church, a capacity crowd listened to three hours of speeches, prayers, and poems. The Handel Society of Portsmouth sang. Gangs of enthusiastic boys set off so many "India crackers" it sounded like the Fourth of July.

That afternoon, 200 invited dignitaries dined on "fish of all known names." Two tables stretched the length of the second floor at Jefferson Hall above the original brick market building. Guests toasted great men, most of them forgotten today, and sang patriotic songs that grew louder and more jubilant as the wine flowed.

It was okay, the struggling businessmen of 1823 told one another, to strive for wealth and success. Hadn't New Hampshire's founder, Captain John Mason, intended to profit from his Strawberry Bank investment? Later generations had grown rich on lumbering, ship-building, and the East India trade. The handsome mansions dotting the compact area of the city were proof of better times. Nathaniel Haven, meanwhile, made no apology for the destruction of indigenous lives and lands, the enslavement of Africans, or the creation of an impoverished working class that could be seen begging in the streets of Portsmouth.

New Hampshire's founders were flawed men and women, Haven admitted, without offering specifics. They were not the sharpest knives in the drawer, he implied, but they were hard-working, God-fearing, and unbreakable. Some were Puritans, some Anglicans, but all were chiseled from sturdy British stock. In 200 years, Haven admitted, Portsmouth had yet to produce any important writers, poets, or painters. But they would come, he promised, in future generations.

The great contradiction of Portsmouth history for Haven and his contemporaries was that many of the city's rich and famous citizens had been loyalists who opposed the American Revolution, not patriots. In the twentieth century, as the city began to develop its tourist trade, nine historic house museums would appear. Each nonprofit museum would promote its colonial owners and early architecture, but also offered patriotic tales when possible. The 1758 Purcell House, for example, once owned by a merchant sea captain, became known for renting rooms to naval hero John Paul Jones.

The most important part of the 1823 bicentennial may have been the "superb ball" held that evening. Some 400 ladies and gentlemen gathered at Franklin Hall further down Congress Street, the site of the Franklin Block today. An unscrolled length of paper bearing the signatures of party guests can be seen on the second floor landing in the Portsmouth Athenaeum. The highlight of the event was the exhibition of about thirty paintings borrowed from local families. One newspaper reported:

> *The walls of the room were entirely covered with portraits of eminent persons who flourished in this state before the revolution—the Wentworths, Jaffreys, Warners, Sparhawks, and Atkinsons of old times.*

The rare display included merchant John Moffatt and his wife. Their colonial mansion, now the Moffatt-Ladd House Museum, was also home to William Whipple, a signer of the Declaration of Independence. A painting of Frances Atkinson Wentworth, arrayed in all her finery, reminded locals of her scandalous marriage to her cousin John. Driven from the city by an angry mob in 1775, Governor John Wentworth and his wife escaped to Nova Scotia. Each painting told a story about the city's faded golden age.

Visitors saw the noble figures of Henry Sherburne, two Wibirds, and two Waldrons. Among them was Reverend Samuel Haven, Nathaniel Haven's grandfather, who had chatted with George Washington at what is now Haven Park. One portrait, painted in 1623, had been shipped to America by family descendants. Another, painted in Scotland, dated to 1555.

For the first time, citizens of the early 1800s came face to face with the wealthy aristocrats who once ruled the town. These were the men, most of them Harvard graduates, who razed the timber forests, built great ships, fought the French, and survived the Indian wars. They were citizens of a king, not the United States. Dressed in fine clothes, striking noble poses, and surrounded by painted possessions, they appeared to live in a foreign land. It was up to their descendants, Haven said, to keep the grandeur of the city's heyday alive.

Daniel Webster recycled his Plymouth speech from three years earlier. "It is wise for us to recur to the history of our ancestors," Webster had said. "Those who do not look upon themselves as a link connecting the Past with the Future, do not perform their duty to the world."

Portsmouth, too, was being marketed as a sacred place where visitors could come to commune with the past. Portsmouth-born historian John Lord, however, was unimpressed with the city's puffed-up image of its brief heyday. "No town in New England," Lord wrote, "claimed to be more aristocratic. In no town was there greater pride in ancestors who were generals and merchants. In no town was society more exclusive and pretentious."

The 1823 portrait gallery was so popular it was briefly opened to the public. Even the city's "lower classes" were given the chance to gawk at the colonial portraits. The bicentennial also inspired the creation of a New Hampshire Historical Society. The nonprofit group, now located in a magnificent granite and marble building not far from the state capitol in Concord, is dedicated to preserving state artifacts, documents, and stories.

"Early nineteenth-century commemoratives were part of the process of history making," says Piscataqua-based scholar Richard M. Candee. These anniversary events were "intended to create regional identity by transforming New England into the moral and cultural center of the nation." Portsmouth, like America, was inventing itself.

Portsmouth's formal toasts, songs, exhibitions, and public procession in 1823 defined both the city's history and its brand. But compared to the well-documented drama of the Pilgrims' self-imposed exile from their homeland, the New Hampshire founding story appeared bland

and uninspiring. Three decades later, teacher and author Edward A. Charlton could scarcely summon enough energy to mention the Piscataqua settlers. "Thus time passed away, presenting but few incidents worthy of note," Charlton wrote in *New Hampshire, As It Is* (1856). "No remarkable events occurred: at least none that have been recorded. . . what toils and sufferings they endured, neither history nor tradition informs us."

From a nineteenth-century perspective, Granite State history was all about Indian raids, Revolutionary War heroes, and Civil War battles. New Hampshire's watery English origins, obscured by time and often embarrassing, were hardly worth mentioning.

CHAPTER 30
Please Come Home

New Hampshire's only seaport has come a long way since the somber celebration of 1823, but slowly. So many Portsmouth men had abandoned their hometown to seek their fortune elsewhere, that the second reunion was held in Boston. On November 7, 1849, New Hampshire expatriates led, once again, by Daniel Webster, spent a month preparing an all-male "Festival of Sons" reunion.

The 1,500 guests, all with ties to New Hampshire, marched through Boston streets to a gaslit hall. Sketches of rural life lined the walls. Goldfish swam in a central fountain. The menu offered a variety of boiled meats, including tongue and "salt-petered beef." Participants enjoyed scalloped oysters, fruity desserts, lemonade, and coffee.

Senator Daniel Webster spoke proudly of New England men who had fought in the French and Indian wars. He praised heroes of the American Revolution. Supreme Court Justice Levi Woodbury, now buried in Portsmouth's South Cemetery, toasted brave men of the Granite State. Speech after speech dripped with nostalgia for New Hampshire—their birth mother, the fatherland, the native state, the alma mater, and the ancient home of the assembled delegates. Rowdy men toasted and cheered late into the night. They recited poems about Old Strawbery Bank, the White Mountains, and New Hampshire's mighty lakes. The 150-page summary, including the names of every participant, reads today like a powerful sedative.

Early in 1853, influential former residents began floating the idea in the Boston press of another reunion. The goal was to lure the "Sons of Portsmouth" back to their home turf on the Fourth of July. The "work of agitation," what we would today call advertising and promotion, hit the media in June. One newspaper poem began: "Come rally boys! Awake, Awake!"

Former New Hampshire sons were invited to join Portsmouth VIPs at "a mammoth chowder" to be served under a tent. Tickets sold quickly, leaving locals feverishly ironing out the details as Independence Day approached.

A hand-tinted illustration shows a towering wooden arch draped with greenery at the Daniel Street opening to Market Square. Welcoming arches appeared at each entrance to the city center. The modern thirty-seven-foot-tall metal arch leading to the Music Hall echoes that tradition. An 1853 poem notes, "The arches, wreathed in living green/ Bent kindly o'er the festive scene."

According to newspaper editor Charles Brewster, a thousand returning sons attended the Portsmouth Jubilee. New Yorkers and residents of a dozen western states showed up two days early. Guests from Boston, Newburyport, Lowell, and other Massachusetts cities arrived via the new Eastern Railroad train. They assembled at "Creek Bridge" in the West End. As in previous events, the men formed a procession based on their occupations—blacksmiths, caulkers, seamen, joiners, painters, cabinet-makers, and more. Marching toward the heart of the city, they passed buildings festooned with colorful banners, flags, evergreens, and flowers. The crackle, clang, and roar of guns, squibs, bells, brass bands, firecrackers, and cheers filled the salt air.

The goal of the Return of the Sons, Brewster wrote, was to revive and increase "the sentiment of local attachment." Such celebrations could inspire patriotism and "strengthen the ties of brotherhood." A full afternoon of speeches, prayers, toasts, and poetry readings was topped off by an open air concert in the setting sun.

The commercially successful jubilee inspired a plan to hold Old Home Day reunions every ten years, but the bloody Civil War intervened. By 1872, a small group had begun testing the public's interest in another Fourth of July homecoming. The year 1873 would be the 250th anniversary of the city's founding.

"While there was no positive opposition to the movement," one observer reported, "there existed the usual amount of apathy which always attends the planning and starting of an enterprise of any great magnitude." But over the winter enthusiasm spread. Volunteers appeared and committees formed to locate speakers, raise funds, send invitations, decorate buildings and streets, build arches, manage the traditional processional, and arrange meals and lodging.

July 4, 1873 was extremely hot and yet the streets were "swarming with humanity." An estimated 25,000 attended, ranging from "the gray-haired sire to the toddling infant." This time, the city made a special effort to honor women as well. With an eye toward future tourism, speakers proclaimed anyone who loved the city, whether born there or not, was now an honorary son or daughter of Portsmouth.

The floats on horse-drawn "cars" were more elaborate than ever. Some, like the display of furniture from the Sheldon Brothers Store, were merely rolling advertisements. The original 1756 printing press of the *New Hampshire Gazette* was on view. A decorative boat on wheels, trimmed with flowers, carried young ladies dressed as Grecian maidens in pink and white gowns.

Like the grand arches strategically placed around town, Portsmouth had one foot planted firmly in the past and another stepping toward the future. Publisher James T. Fields, born in the South End of the city and married to popular writer Annie Fields, spoke openly of the need for change.

"The men of the world have not until quite recently begun to deal out even-handed justice to the women of the world," Fields said. "And even now, many of us hang back. . . I fully believe that a new era of happiness is waiting to dawn on that portion of the earth where woman shall be thoroughly educated, not ornamented only, and where minds shall be equal and triumphantly crowned without any regard to sex."

The celebration did not entirely ignore its prime mover. In the final pages of a souvenir book, *The Re-Union of '73*, publisher Charles W. Gardner mentioned the "good, honest, reputable yeoman" who first set up their fish flakes at Odiorne Point. But the "three days carnival," Gardner admitted, had largely overshadowed its historical origins.

A few weeks after the festivities, a group of gentlemen met in the city chamber and unanimously agreed to fund a memorial. The Little Harbor monument "should be of height and breadth sufficient to be seen from the ocean, that is, it should be of a respectable size, if not imposing." Although a "considerable outlay" would be required for construction, Gardner was certain, "So excellent an undertaking cannot fail to be popular." But the project sank like a stone. Despite another Return of the Sons celebration in 1883, it would be a quarter century before talk of a Thompson memorial resurfaced.

That memorial, such as it is, still stands. The job fell to the National Society of Colonial Dames of America in the State of New Hampshire. Erected in the final weeks of the nineteenth-century on a bluff overlooking Little Harbor, the grim granite monument has the haunting shape of a cemetery stone and bears the dates "1623-1899." It honors "the first band of Englishmen Pioneers" who settled New Hampshire. In his 1899 dedicatory address, Concord minister Joseph B.Walker repeated the local legend that Odiorne Point represents the third British settlement in America after Jamestown and New Plymouth. But unlike many of his colleagues, Walker was up-to-date on the research by Charles Deane, John Scribner Jenness, and Frank W. Hackett.

"According to the latest authorities to which I have had access,"

Walker explained, David Thompson had likely picked Little Harbor due to the active fishing operation at the Isles of Shoals. Thompson had moved on after three years, died of an unknown cause, and no remnants of his Pannaway outpost had survived. While praising the Colonial Dames for their patriotic effort, Walker regretted that fading interest in early New Hampshire history had resulted in a much less dramatic memorial than originally planned.

The group then joined in a rousing version of "Keller's American Hymn." The Civil War battle song by German immigrant Matthias Keller seems an incongruous choice for a peaceful seaside memorial to a colonial fishing outpost. They sang:

> *Foremost in battle, for Freedom to stand,*
> *We rush to arms when aroused by its call;*
> *Still as of yore when George Washington led,*
> *Thunders our war-cry, We conquer or fall!*

As the 1899 ceremony concluded, Reverend Joseph Walker wrapped up his eulogy. "Hail, and hail again; to the monument which you now unveil!" he shouted into the late October breeze. "Century after century may it firmly stand," he announced, "and connect with a lengthening bond the receding past and the advancing future!"

But in 1955, due to erosion along the fragile seacoast, the First Settlers Monument was moved. Through the rest of the twentieth century it was stored across Route 1A at what may be New Hampshire's oldest graveyard. Then in June 2007, it left Old Odiorne Point Cemetery and was returned to its original site. Members of the Odiorne family attended the rededication ceremony. Their ancestors had farmed the land in the 1600s. Centuries later, the federal government seized the Odiorne property under eminent domain to build Fort Dearborn during World War II. Despite efforts to reclaim their ancestral farm, it is now Odiorne State Park.

CHAPTER 31

Party On, Portsmouth!

By the end of the nineteenth century, Portsmouth was addicted to pomp. Early Kodak candids show downtown streets jammed with marching bands and rows of uniformed men. Most notable were parades honoring Civil War veterans, firemen, and labor unions. The Portsmouth Treaty parade of 1905 welcomed delegates from Russia and Japan whose meetings halted an horrific war.

By the Return of the Sons and Daughters in 1910, the city had its party hat permanently glued on. Decorative arches again stretched across key streets. One sign read simply, "COME HOME!" City officials sported blue badges, while the ballooning media wore white. The public carried yellow tickets shaped like keys to the city. The 1910 celebration began with another "grand military and civic parade." Civil War veterans placed a wreath at the Soldiers and Sailors Monument on Islington Street. Then came sporting events, evening concerts, and the inevitable fireworks display.

These frequent celebrations did much more than reunite old friends, fill hotel beds, hawk souvenirs, and sell countless barrels of beer. In an era before radio, TV, and movies, parades were both mass entertainment and a means of social expression. In a tradition dating to the guilds of medieval Europe, men bore icons of their trade. There were barbers in fresh white coats. Coal industry teamsters, shoe workers, box makers, brewers, bottlers, typographers, and laundry workers marched with their fellow tradesmen.

Elaborate horse-drawn floats represented the Hebrew Society, the Italian Orders, and the Colored Fraternities. The Massasoit Society of Red Men (a white male fraternal group) staged an "Indian tableau" complete with feathered headdresses. The Knights of Columbus, another fraternal group, offered a mythological scene of Christopher Columbus discovering America. Marchers representing the Colored Knights of Pythias joined the Masons, Odd Fellows, Elks, church groups, and school children.

Two all-but-forgotten figures helped raise the Portsmouth parade to an art form. Thomas P. Moses, a talented but temperamental teacher, painter, and church organist, held "floral concerts." His unique blend of sacred and popular music, combined with exquisite displays of flowers and greenery, caught on in a city more familiar with saloons, spittoons, and bordellos.

Nineteenth-century Portsmouth bookseller James Head was another floral architect. Head created a how-to guide with 150 sketches for creating attractive parade floats, arches, and monuments. His unpublished manuscript rests in the vault at the Portsmouth Athenaeum. His illustrations included tableaux vivant or "living pictures" in which costumed figures posed in historic, biblical, and patriotic scenes. James Head and Thomas Moses encouraged neighbors to join forces to decorate streets and buildings, to perform in public, and to share messages embedded in public celebrations.

Their spirit culminated at the city's over-the-top tercentennial. The 1923 parade featured a huge tall ship on wheels and an equally large Liberty Bell promoting the new Bell Telephone Company. The local chapter of the Ku Klux Klan offered a floral display picturing the Declaration of Independence and the U.S. Constitution.

Portsmouth's city fathers wisely hired Virginia Tanner to stage an unforgettable 300th anniversary event. Tanner was a renowned pageant designer, actress, dancer, and author from Cambridge, Massachusetts.

Born in 1881, she held a master's degree from Radcliffe College. She was also a friend of the famed Boston Impressionist painter, Edmund C. Tarbell, who summered in nearby New Castle.

Her job, Tanner wrote in the introduction to a *Pageant of Portsmouth* souvenir booklet, was "to ransack the dusty shelves" of local history and make the past meaningful. Tanner selected events that spectators could see and appreciate at night, under lights, without dialogue, and at a great distance.

A hundred women sewed the costumes. A hundred sopranos sang in the chorus. Tanner ordered wigs shipped from New York. Professional dancers came from the National Ballet in Washington, DC. Thousands attended the three-day Portsmouth pageant in an outdoor arena known as The Pines, just off South Street. A woman draped in the diaphanous costume of a goddess welcomed the gathering. The "Spirit of Portsmouth" was attended by similarly dressed women representing Rye, Greenland, New Castle, Newington, Kittery, and the Isles of Shoals.

No woman dressed in an ancient tunic or "peplos" represented Dover in the Portsmouth celebration that year. The two towns had been feuding over their 1623 founding date since the bicentennial of 1823. Not to be outdone, Dover simultaneously staged its own elaborate tercentennial pageant narrated by a character dressed as Father Time. A production company from Ohio was hired to stage the Dover Pageant. In a river mill town of only 13,000 residents, an estimated 20,000 attended the event at Dover Point, miles from the town center.

In a detailed study of the Dover Pageant published in 2022, scholars Meghan C. L. Howey and Christine M. DeLucia noted that the location established an "authenticity of place." The pageant drew renewed attention to Hilton's Point (Dover Point), now a public waterfront park, picnic spot, and boat launch. The selected site helped cement the myth of the 1623 Hilton landing into town history.

The pageant portrayed Indians as hostiles who, having failed to rebuff the European founders, had vanished from history. A crude wooden fort constructed for the event was torched and burned during the performance by Dover residents dressed as Indians. According to the study, the event also emphasized the "purity of English identity reckoned through genealogical descent." Prominent citizens, the pageant creators implied, were those most closely descended from the town's first English settlers. A century later, by contrast, Dover's 400th celebration in 2023 openly acknowledged its debt to Native people of the past and present day.

Back in Portsmouth, Tanner's 1923 chorus sang as electric lamps illuminated a tree-lined field. Over the next few hours, a thousand re-enactors pantomimed the city's history. The timeline stretched from the arrival of explorers Martin Pring and Captain John Smith through the royal Wentworth dynasty, to the storied visits by Paul Revere, John Paul Jones, and George Washington. A "colored chorus" of Black residents sang spirituals. Immigrants from the city's Polish, Irish, Italian, Greek, and Chinese families were also highlighted.

The event grossed $11,388, plus the sale of souvenir booklets. Virginia Tanner received a respectable $2,000, roughly $36,000 today. The *Portsmouth Herald* called her pageant "a dazzling, inspiring spectacle." Back in 1823, the city had come to terms with its founding as a commercial enterprise. But by 1923, the Colonial Revival and the beloved Thanksgiving holiday had done their work. One of Tanner's Portsmouth Tercentennial posters featured a swarm of musket-toting Puritans arriving at the Piscataqua by ship. The leader, with his tall buckled hat and buckled shoes waved in greeting as two shadowy Indian figures in the foreground welcomed the colonists ashore.

Tanner went on to stage similar events in other New England towns. But the golden age of American pageantry faded from the American scene after the arrival of talking films in the late 1920s. Watching movies alone in a darkened cinema was so much easier than working with neighbors to build floats and arches, march in grand parades, and stage live exhibitions. In Portsmouth, however, the pageantry continued.

Fast forward fifty years. On May 18, 1973, Governor Meldrim Thomson, Jr. officially acknowledged New Hampshire's 350th birthday. Portsmouth Mayor Arthur Brady kicked off a weeklong city celebration. The traditional parade was organized by the "Piscataqua Bucks" and the "Piscataqua Belles." A scaled-down pageant took place under the stars at the high school athletic field.

"They Came to Fish" reprised the city's glorious and inglorious moments. The *Portsmouth Herald* described the outdoor performance as "a fairly accurate portrayal" of the past. More than a thousand opening night spectators witnessed Sagamore Passaconaway making peace with white settlers. David Thompson arrived at Odiorne Point. Ruth Blay, an eighteenth-century teacher, was hanged in South Cemetery for concealing the birth of her stillborn child. Stamp Act protestors rioted and bucket brigades fought downtown fires. In a whimsical scene, Portsmouth's vintage baseball team battled "those dirty rotten cheats from Dover." (Old grudges die hard.) Pageant sponsors awarded winners of the "350th Queen Contest" with a Singer sewing machine, a Zenith portable TV, a Bulova diamond watch, and a Clairol make-up mirror.

It was during the 1973 anniversary that Matthew E. Thompson, a retired Navy commander and math professor from Oregon, visited Portsmouth with a stirring message. The amateur historian, then in his seventies, told the *Portsmouth Herald* that New Hampshire could turn its historical calendar back to 1622. Based on his family history, Thompson claimed, an advance team backed by Sir Ferdinando Gorges and John Mason had set up a fortified structure at Odiorne Point one year before David Thompson and his family arrived. The theory, Matthew Thompson told the newspaper, was the result of research by his brother Ralph, a retired civil engineer from New Jersey. The Thompson brothers' fifty-page treatise, later developed into the book *First Yankee*, declared Little Harbor was once the "de facto capital of New England."

Although no evidence supports their 1622 theory, the Thompson brothers had a point. Based on British records, the New Hampshire seacoast predated Massachusetts as the regional seat of government. It didn't last long, but the idea created a ripple of interest among local history buffs. If nothing else, it reminded us that the Puritan domination of New England was not a foregone conclusion.

We owe the Thompson brothers our gratitude for dragging their supposed ancestor back into the limelight during one of those rare anniversary years when the entire city turns its attention to history. They also identified London as the birthplace of David Thompson and confirmed that his son, John, was born in England, not on the New Hampshire frontier.

By the time their treatise was expanded and published in 1979, Ralph Thompson had died. In his dedication to *First Yankee*, Matthew noted their study began soon after the deaths of their beloved wives. "We two septuagenarians found solace in genealogical research," Matthew confessed. The book was a gift to their children and grandchildren. But what began as a search for the truth spiraled into the realm of wishful thinking that, today, is too often taken for fact.

"I was sometimes bogged down and discouraged," the author added. "I am not overly happy with the product, but at least it is done. Somebody ought to tell the story of that remarkable woman, Amias (Cole) Thomson Maverick." Amen to that and, hopefully, what we know about her has come to life in these pages.

The city's 375th anniversary caught Portsmouth by surprise. In 1998, Mayor Evelyn Sirrell hastily assembled a Blue Ribbon Committee to memorialize the date. A classy logo, souvenir history booklet, exhibits, lectures, T-shirts, a 5K race, and parade soon appeared. But a much anticipated visit by the tall ship "Old Ironsides" did not. Nor were the tattered remnants of the city's Old State House rebuilt, as many hoped. The Portsmouth Historical Society buried a large plastic time capsule that won't see the light of day until 2123.

The big anniversaries, however, are the ones with two zeroes. Learning from the past, planners began discussing the city's quadricentennial far in advance. Under the direction of the Portsmouth Historical Society, by 2017 work was already underway. Plans called for an "inclusive celebration" to explore the region's diverse heritage beginning before the first European settlers arrived. "We will not just blow out the candles in 2023!" one organizer promised. A steering committee was formed, public forums were held, and a full-time 400th director was appointed. Portsmouth was enjoying an economic boom. All things seemed possible—until a worldwide pandemic put the planet on hold.

Suddenly it was mid-2021. With the historic year now threatening, a 400th reboot was initiated. A new nonprofit group linked to the city government took over. Divided into seven thematic "pillars," PortsmouthNH400, Inc. became a clearinghouse for scores of independently created anniversary projects. Assembling a calendar of events was no problem for a tourist town already buzzing with exhibitions, concerts, galleries, performances, lectures, tours, cruises, street fairs, gift shops, historic sites, pubs, and eateries.

The 2023 "Signature Events" included a Grand Parade and a carnival in memory of "Little Italy," a lost neighborhood bulldozed by urban renewal half a century ago. Two weeks later the 400th committee staged a spectacular outdoor dinner. Despite threatening weather, 900 diners gathered around a table stretching five blocks down the center of Congress Street. Amid speeches, live music, and a laser lightshow, the crowd consumed lobsters, chicken, and corn on the cob. "This is the party!" sponsors told the *Portsmouth Herald,* and indeed it was. In a possible nod to David Thompson's short-lived business, organizers advertised the event as "celebrating commerce and community since 1623." No one mentioned that both Little Harbor and Strawberry Bank investors failed to make a nickel.

Back at Odiorne Point in Rye, near the boat launch where our story began, a subtle but significant change took place. Early in the summer of 2023, the historic marker bearing the official New Hampshire state seal disappeared. For decades the plaque had indicated David Thompson came from England "to colonize," a term increasingly associated today with an invading force. The sign also incorrectly named his son, John, as the first English child born in what would become the Granite State. A new historic marker offers an updated message. It begins:

This seaside place is located on N'dakinna, the traditional homeland of the Abenaki, Pennacook, and Wabanaki People, past and present. In 1623, David Thompson settled here to fish, farm, and trade under a grant from the British Council for New England, displacing the Native peoples.

Were the seventeenth-century Thompsons brave adventurers, pioneering entrepreneurs, or an invasive species? Rarely mentioned and still misunderstood, they gave New Hampshire its founding date, then disappeared. Their complex story, like so much of our national narrative, deserves a fresh look.

EPILOGUE

Epilogue: Updating the Past

D oes what happened here in 1623 matter to us today? I truly believe it does. When I first met David Thompson fifty years ago, he was a minor character in a book pulled randomly from a library shelf. Pilgrim leader Edward Winslow had mentioned Thompson in his journal, *Good News from New England*. When Winslow's book was published in London in 1624, Thompson was depicted as little more than a "Scotchman" and a fish merchant settling in at Little Harbor "where he liketh well."

But Thompson was much more than a guy who delivered seafood to starving Pilgrims. The more I dug into the story over the decades, the more important he became. As an Anglican agent for John Mason and Ferdinando Gorges, Thompson was a potentially threatening figure to the Pilgrims. Like the Separatists, he had not come alone, but brought his wife and child to the wilderness, clearly intending to stay. He held an official grant from the Council for New England. He had a shallop, a sturdy house, and a small workforce. He was an educated man of medicine. In 1623, having just arrived, Thompson was already the owner of a busy stopping point for important visitors of every status, from Phineas Pratt to Christopher Levett and the Pilgrims themselves.

The Thompsons sheltered and clothed the duplicitous Thomas Weston. They sponsored the ceremony that made Robert Gorges the first governor of all New England. And then, ramping up the threat to New Plymouth, they moved south from Pascataquack to Boston Harbor and took possession of a fertile island at what was clearly the best site to build an English nation. And when Robert Gorges died, wasn't David Thompson the acting governor of the entire region under the authority of the king?

David's undocumented disappearance at this precise moment in history has always troubled me. I believe in coincidences, not conspiracy theories, but I couldn't help taunting Plimoth Plantation reenactor Scott Atwood when I interviewed him a dozen years ago. Atwood was then performing as Miles Standish at the living history museum in Massachusetts. Frozen in time, it is always 1627 at the reconstructed Pilgrim village. When "in character," the well-trained actors appear to know nothing of the future provinces of Massachusetts or New Hampshire. If you mention the word "computer," for example, the actor might say, "Yes, we have some pewter too!"

Besides appearing in countless thousands of tourist photos and films, Atwood played his part in TV documentaries, travel brochures, and lectures. During school visits, he wore a hat when performing as Standish. Removing his hat transformed the actor back into Scott Atwood, allowing him to comment from a twenty-first century perspective. I interviewed both men, past and present, who did not always agree with one another.

When I asked if the Pilgrims had any news of the disappearance of David Thompson, Atwood replied, "I don't think we want to get into that." His alter ego then took over.

"Show me the body!" Standish thundered, sparked by my not-too-subtle insinuation.

Atwood, the role player, cautioned me that in 1627, even suggesting that Standish might be involved in a murder plot was against the law. I could be arrested, put on trial, and banished from the colony—or worse. What some call the Wessagusset massacre, Atwood explained, was more of a "pre-emptive strike" against a group of Natives during dangerous times.

Standish, his blood rising, then reeled off a list of suspects. What about Roger Conant at Cape Ann or Samuel Maverick on Noddles Island? Anyone might have harbored a grudge against Thompson, including the ferocious "savages," he said. I took a risk and asked the fiery captain if he thought Thompson might have met with foul play.

"Who's suggesting it, and what sort of slander is that?" Standish shouted, gripping the hilt of his imaginary sword.

Atwood gestured for me to back off. The hot-tempered military leader never forgets a grudge. Any more questions, he warned, and the Captain might suddenly take action against me.

"And then it will out!" Standish shouted, brandishing his weapon. I got the hint and quickly exited the year 1627, leaving David Thompson's disappearance an unsolved mystery.

In the half century I've been studying the Thompsons, our collective view of the nation's past has evolved. Sports teams and schools are finally replacing mascots based on offensive ethnic and racial stereotypes. Civil War monuments dedicated to men who fought to preserve slavery are coming down. The Portsmouth Black Heritage Trail and the African American Burying Ground Memorial are now must-see destinations in New Hampshire. Last year the city officially discarded Christopher Columbus and adopted Indigenous Peoples' Day. The Portsmouth Historical Society offers a downtown walking tour dedicated entirely to influential women. Fresh new biographies, history documentaries, websites, and podcasts are re-examining our founding legends and fleshing out forgotten figures.

Nowhere is the tricky balance between preserving and updating the past more evident than at the living history museum created in 1947 as Plimoth Plantation. Plimoth, like Old Sturbridge Village, Colonial Williamsburg, and later Strawbery Banke Museum, was born in a burst of postwar patriotism. By this time, the *Mayflower* journey had become a staple tale in educational books for young readers. The

narrative, echoing the Old Testament, framed the exodus of a persecuted people. In short, children were taught, the Pilgrims were a band
of near-flawless heroes who tamed a godless wilderness and birthed a
democratic new nation. To follow their example, kids were instructed
in the benefits of hard work, self sacrifice and Christian piety.

In 2001, Plimoth launched a museum-wide effort, based on
modern scholarship, to reimagine the first harvest fest. In a slim
companion book for children entitled *1621: A New Look at Thanksgiving,*
the authors admit the museum initially left out the perspective of the
Wampanoag people who had lived in the region for thousands of years.

Our modern Thanksgiving holiday, the book notes, is partially
based on fiction. The message for young people is so carefully worded,
however, that it might pass unnoticed. It reads: "Unquestioning accep-
tance of biased interpretations can affect the way we treat one another,
even today." In other words, hundreds of years of trivializing, demon-
izing, and misrepresenting indigenous people might color how we view
them. You think? In fact, later colonists often held "thanksgiving" celebrations after they had defeated Native Americans in battles. Many
indigenous people and their supporters have traded in the traditional
Thanksgiving holiday and replaced it with a day of mourning and
reflection.

We're not here to take away your cranberry sauce. The historian's goal is not to destroy Thanksgiving or any other holiday. We need
our legends and the traditions they engender. That may be especially
true in a young nation scarcely 250 years old. The job of history is to
separate legend from fact. William Bradford, for example, is a great
documentary source for his personal view of life among the Pilgrims.
But as the late Harvard historian Bernard Bailyn reminds us, Bradford
was also the "great mythographer."

"We live with the fallout of that mythology," Linda Coombs told
guests at a C-SPAN2 roundtable discussion filmed at Plimoth Plantation

in 2001. A member of the Aquinnah Wampanoag tribe from Martha's Vineyard, Coombs said: "A lot of times Native people feel that Thanksgiving, as we know it today, is done at our expense. . . . We died so that the English could come here and establish a colony."

Governor Bradford would be outraged at the way Thanksgiving is celebrated today, according to John Kemp, a long-time interpreter and administrator at Plimoth. Kemp moderated the C-SPAN2 meeting and boldly stated, "What is done in modern America in the name of Thanksgiving has nothing to do with the view of thanksgiving in colonial times."

A veteran role player at Plimoth, Kemp noted that Bradford's view of history should be deployed with care. "There's some very very inhumane writing, if to you, inhumane means having a disrespect for humanity," Kemp said. Bradford and his Separatist band believed "England was the leading nation of the Lord's people" and their beliefs were superior to all others, including Natives, Catholics, Jews, all non-Christians.

"Many people are surprised to hear this," Kemp added. "They [Pilgrims] did not come for religious freedom. If you were a Baptist, or a Quaker, or some other kind of Protestant that was not in line with the Puritan view of the true religion—you were not welcome here. There was persecution in Plymouth Colony right from the early years."

David Silverman, a professor of history at The George Washington University, told the *Boston Globe* that the popular outdoor history museum has a tough needle to thread.

"I don't envy their leadership," he said in 2020. "They can't win. If they tell the people the story, warts and all, few people will pay to bring their kids there."

"Honest history offends just about everybody," Silverman added. "The seventeenth century was a brutal time. At any given time, you'd walk into Plymouth Colony and there would be several Native heads outside the gate. You could walk into a Wampanoag community and see scalps flying over a residence. It's a barbaric time by our standards. Not for family consumption."

Two centuries after Daniel Webster turned Plymouth into a patriotic shrine, "America's Hometown" was gearing up for a torrent of tourists. But Covid quashed the 400-year celebration. In 2020, to become more inclusive, the popular outdoor history attraction dropped the word "plantation" from its name. It has been rebranded as Plimoth Patuxet Museums.

The Patuxet were a Native American band of the Wampanoag tribal confederation. They were largely wiped out by the diseases brought by European explorers prior to the landing of the *Mayflower*. Tisquantum, the storied Native (better known as "Squanto") who assisted the Pilgrims, is often considered the last survivor of the Patuxet. It is his lost village that is being reimagined by indigenous educators at the museum today. So I guess we are making progress.

The good news is that some Americans are coming to terms with the complex reality behind the romanticized Thanksgiving holiday. Annual media coverage now delights in comparing our modern November feast with what was likely on the menu at New Plymouth in 1621. The perception that *Mayflower* passengers were the first European arrivals to New England is slowly being erased. Tales of the Pilgrims living in harmony with indigenous people, or kick-starting American democracy with the Mayflower Compact, or landing at Plymouth Rock are being counterbalanced by factual reporting.

Looking back, my fascination with the Thompsons was certainly grounded in a growing disenchantment with the Pilgrim legend I learned at school in the 1950s and 1960s. My New Hampshire high school students in the 1970s and 1980s knew nothing much beyond Plymouth Rock and pumpkin pie. Then in 1995, James W. Loewen released his eye-opening *Lies My Teacher Told Me*. His examination of a dozen high school history texts found them filled with "false, Eurocentric, and mythologized views of American history." Loewen found the heroification of the Pilgrims and the Puritans who followed to be downright dangerous. Reverend John Winthrop's Shining City had morphed into a belief that America was not only exceptional, but superior in every way to all other nations.

I was, by then, a full-time writer. It was Loewen, in part, who convinced me to focus on local history in what, so far, adds up to roughly 3,000 published articles and over a dozen books. The goal here is not to cancel the Pilgrims, but rather to remind us that the cuddly characters we grew up with were not the Separatists of the 1620s. David and Amias Thompson offer us, not alternate heroes, but a reality check into a very different, often dark, and largely forgotten era.

"My book is hardly the first to trouble the Puritan myth," Joseph Kelly writes in *Marooned*, his modern rethinking of Jamestown Colony. "Debunking Pilgrims is something of a cottage industry." But this work is necessary, Kelly says, to counterbalance the widespread notion that the journals of Bradford and Winslow are "the sacred texts of the American people" and "the root of American values."

And it's not just a Pilgrim problem. The more we return indigenous voices into our founding story, the more sense it makes. The same happens when we include the lives of Africans, of immigrants of all races and religions, of the poor, the marginalized, the young, and of women. I own a six-volume hardcover history of New Hampshire written in the twentieth century. It includes full-page portraits of 100 important Granite State figures. Only one of them is a woman.

Where to from here? Let's agree not to build statues of David and Amias Thompson, wrap their lives in fairy tales, then knock the statues down. But, come on, New Hampshire! Let's not forget them. They are the portal to a much needed re-examination of how New England happened.

Select Bibliography

Adams, Charles Francis, Jr. (editor). *The New English Canaan of Thomas Morton*. Boston: The Prince Society, 1883.

——. *Three Episodes of Massachusetts History*. Boston: Houghton, Mifflin and Company, 1892.

——. *Wessagusset and Weymouth, An Historical Address*. Weymouth Historical Society, 1905.

Adams, James Ring. "Alien Abduction: How the Abenaki Discovered England." *American Indian* vol. 16, no. 3 (Fall 2015).

Agricola, Gerogius (translated by Herbert Clark Hoover). *De Re Metallica (On the Nature of Metals)*. London: The Mining Magazine, 1912. (originally 1556, first book brought to Strawberry Bank Colony)

Anderson, Robert Charles. *The Great Migration Begins: Immigrants to New England 1620-1633*. Boston: New England Historic Genealogical Society, six volumes, 1995-2001.

Anonymous. *The Re-union of '73: The Second Reception of the Sons and Daughters of Portsmouth*. Portsmouth, NH: Charles W. Gardner, 1873.

Anonymous. "King James and the Council of New England." *Historical New Hampshire*, April 1948.

Apothecaries Hall. *"Origins: The Worshipful Society of Apothecaries."* Apothecaries.org.

Aspinwall, William. *"A Volume Relating to the Early History of Boston Containing the Aspinwall Notarial Records from 1644 to 1651."* Boston: Boston Registry Department, 1903. (includes indenture of Thompson's Plymouth apartment)

Bailyn, Bernard. *Barbarous Years: The Peopling of British North America: The Conflict of Civilizations, 1600-1675*. New York: Vintage Books, 2013.

Baker, Emerson W. "Trouble to the Eastward: The Failure of Anglo-Indian Relations in Early Maine" (1986). *Dissertations, Theses, and Masters Projects.* William & Mary.

Baker, Emerson W., Nina N. Maurer, and Old Berwick Historical Society. *Forgotten Frontier: Untold Stories of the Piscataqua.* South Berwick, Maine: Old Berwick Historical Society, 2018.

Baxter, James Phinney and Christopher Levett. *Christopher Levett, of York, the Pioneer Colonist in Casco Bay.* Portland, Maine: Printed for the Gorges Society, 1893.

Baxter, James Phinney. *Sir Ferdinando Gorges and His Province of Maine.* Boston: Published for the Prince Society, 1890.

Beals, Carelton. "The Rebels of Merry Mount," *American Heritage,* June 1955.

Belknap, Jeremy (John Farmer, editor). *The History of New Hampshire.* United States: S. C. Stevens and Ela & Wadleigh, 1831. (reprint of 1784 original)

Benedict, W.H.W. "Roberts Farm for 300 Years Passed from Father to Son." *Boston Sunday Globe,* September 9, 1928.

Blackhawk, Ned. *The Rediscovery of America: Native Peoples and the Unmaking of U.S. History.* New Haven and London: Yale University Press, 2023.

Blake, James. *Annals of the Town of Dorchester, 1750.* Boston: Dave Clapp, Jr., 1846.

Bolton, Charles Knowles. *The Real Founders of New England: Stories of Their Life Along the Coast, 1602-1628.* Boston: F. W. Faxon Co., 1929.

BookTV C-SPAN2. *"1621: A New Look at Thanksgiving."* November 6, 2001. C-SPAN.org (book discussion video online)

Bouton, Nathaniel, DD (editor). *Provincial Papers: Documents and Records Relating to the Province of New Hampshire from the Earliest Period of Its Settlement 1623-1686.* Concord: George E. Jenks, State Printer, 1867.

Bradford, William. *Governor William Bradford's Letter Book.* Bedford, MA: Applewood Books, 2012 reprint. (excellent introduction by John C. Kemp)

———. (Worthington Chauncey Ford, editor). *History of Plymouth Plantation, 1620-1647.* Boston: The Massachusetts Historical Society, 1912. (reprint)

———. (Samuel Eliot Morison, editor). *Of Plymouth Plantation, 1620-1647.* United States: Knopf, 1952. (reprint)

Bradley, Charles Henry. *Thompson's Island and the Farm and Trades School.* Boston: University of Massachusetts, (Farm and Trade School Press), 1909.

Brewster, Charles Warren. *Rambles About Portsmouth: Sketches of Persons, Localities, and Incidents of Two Centuries, Principally from Tradition and Unpublished Documents.* Somersworth, NH: New Hampshire Pub. Co., 1972. (two-volume reprint of 1869 and 1873 editions)

Burrage, Henry Sweetser. *Gorges and the Grant of the Province of Maine, 1622: A Tercentenary Manual.* State of Maine, 1923.

Butman, John. "Sir Ferdinando Gorges and His Impossible Dream of Maine," *MaineBoats.com*

Candee, Richard M. "The 1823 'Centennial' Celebration of New Hampshire's Settlement." New England Celebrates: Spectacle, Commemoration, and Festivity: *The Dublin Seminar for New England Folklife Annual Proceedings*, June 2000. Boston: Boston University, 2002.

Cartier, Craig S. "An Investigation into Weston's Colony in Wessagusset." Plymouth Archaeological Rediscovery Project. March 2011, *plymoutharch.com*

Center for the History of Medicine at Countway Library Collections. "Who Were the Apothecaries?" *countway.harvard.edu*

Chamberlain, Mellen., William Richard Cutter, Jenny Chamberlain Watts. *A Documentary History of Chelsea: Including the Boston Precincts of Winnisimmet, Rumney Marsh, and Pullen Point, 1624-1824.* United States: Massachusetts Historical Society, 1908.

Charlton, Edwin A. *New Hampshire As It Is.* Bowie, MD: Heritage Books Inc., 1997. (originally 1855, published in Claremont, NH)

Churchill, E.A. "A Most Ordinary Lot of Men: Tte Fishermen at Richmond Island, Maine, in the Early Seventeenth Century." *The New England Quarterly* vol. 57, no. 2 (June, 1984): 184-204.

Clark, Charles E. *Maine: A History*. New York: W.W. Norton & Company, Inc., 1977.

———. *The Eastern Frontier: The Settlement of Northern New England*. New York: Alfred A. Knopf, 1970.

Crosby, Howard S., Wendy W. Lull, and Richard T. MacIntyre. *Footprints in Time: A Walk Where New Hampshire Began*. Bath: A. Sutton, 1994.

Cummins, Sharon. "Winter Harbor Settled Before Plymouth," *Portsmouth Herald*, May 29, 2008.

Daniell, Jere R. *Colonial New Hampshire: A History*. United States: KTO Press, 1981.

Dean, John Ward (editor) and Charles Wesley Tuttle. *Capt. John Mason: The Founder of New Hampshire*. Boston: The Prince Society, 1887.

Deane, Charles. *Notes on a Recently Discovered Indenture Relating to David Thomson of Piscataqua and Massachusetts*. Cambridge, MA: Press of John Wilson and Son, 1876.

Deane, Charles (editor for the publishing committee at the American Antiquarian Society). *Records of the Council for New England*. Cambridge: Press of John Wilson and Son, 1867.

Delaney, Sean. *"Transatlantic Print Culture and the Rise of New England Literature 1620-1630."* Department of History Northeastern University, Boston, MA, April 2013.

Dewar, David. "'The Mason Patents: Conflict, Controversy, and the Quest For Authority in Colonial New Hampshire." *Constructing Early Modern Empires: Proprietary Ventures in the Atlantic World, 1500-1750*. Netherlands: Brill, 2007.

Dymond, Dorothy. *"Captain John Mason and the Duke of Buckingham."* Portsmouth, UK: Portsmouth City Council (Portsmouth Papers no. 17), 1972.

Fagan, Brian M. *Fish on Friday: Feasting, Fasting, and the Discovery of the New World*. New York: Basic Books, 2006.

Fassett, James H. *Colonial Life in New Hampshire*. Boston: Ginna & Company, 1899.

Fischer, David Hackett. *Albion's Seed: Four British Folkways in America*. New York: Oxford University Press, 1989.

Flanders, Mildred Glawson. *Land of the Free: A Pioneer Story for Children*. Northern Publishing House, 1949.

Fraser, Genevieve Cora. "David Thomson, the Scottish Founder of New Hampshire." Massachusetts: *Wellswooster.com*

——. "David Thomson's Letter to the Earl of Arundel." *Wellswooster.com*

Gevitz, Norman. "'Pray Let the Medicines Be Good': The New England Apothecary in the Seventeenth and Early Eighteenth Centuries." *Pharmacy in History,* University of Wisconsin Press vol. 41, no. 3 (1999): 87-101.

Gill, Crispin. *Plymouth: A New History from 1603 to the Present Day*. London: David & Charles, 1979.

Goodall, Felicity. *Lost Plymouth: Hidden Heritage of Three Towns*. Edinburgh: Birlinn, 2009.

Goodwin, John Abbot. *The Pilgrim Republic: An Historical Review of the Colony of New Plymouth, with Sketches of the Rise of Other New England Settlements, the History of Congregationalism, and the Creeds of the Period*. Boston: Ticknor and Company, 1888.

Grace, Catherine O'Neill, Margaret M. Bruchac, Sisse Brimberg, Cotton Coulson, and Plimoth Plantation Inc. *1621: A New Look at Thanksgiving*. Washington, DC: National Geographic Society, 2004.

Hackett, Frank W. *1645-1656, Portsmouth Records, A Transcript of the First Thirty-five Pages of the Earliest Town Book, Portsmouth, New Hampshire: with Notes*. Portsmouth: Privately Printed, 1886.

——. "The Widow of David Thomson," *The New England Historical and Genealogical Register* vol. 47, 1893.

Hamilton, William B. "A Review: Gorges of Plymouth Fort: A Life of Sir Ferdinando Gorges, Captain of Plymouth Fort, Governor of New England, and Lord of the Province of Maine." By Richard Arthur Preston. *The Mississippi Valley Historical Review* 41, no. 4 (1955): 686–87.

Hammond, Otis Grant. "*The Mason Title and Its Relations to New Hampshire and Massachusetts.*" Worcester: American Antiquarian Society, 1910.

Harness, Cheryl. *The Adventurous Life of Myles Standish and the Amazing-But-True Survival Story of Plymouth Colony.* Washington, DC: National Geographic, 2009.

Haubrich, Alice. "Early History of the New Hampshire Settlements," *The Genealogical Record* vol. 13, no.3 (May/June 1990).

Haven, Samuel Foster. *History of Grants Under the Great Council for New England: A Lecture of a Course by Members of the Massachusetts Historical Society, Delivered Before the Lowell Institute, Jan. 15, 1869.* United States: Press of J. Wilson and Son, 1869.

Head, James, H. *Home Pasttimes or Tableaux Vivant.* Boston: J.E. Tilton and Company. 1860.

Heath, William. "Thomas Morton: From Merry Old England to New England." *Journal of American Studies* 41, no. 1 (2007): 135–68.

Hervey, Mary Frederica Sophia. *The Life, Correspondence & Collections of Thomas Howard, Earl of Arundel.* United Kingdom: The University Press, 1921. (includes David Thompson 1625 letter)

Horn, James. *1619: Jamestown and the Forging of American Democracy.* New York: Basic Books, 2018.

Howey, M.C. and C.M. DeLucia. "Spectacles of Settler Colonial Memory: Archaeological Findings from an Early Twentieth-Century 'First' Settlement Pageant and Other Commemorative Terrain in New England." *International Journal of Historical Archaeology,* January 2022. (on the Dover 1923 celebration)

Hubbard, William. *A General History of New England from the Discovery to MDCLXXX.* Boston: Charles C. Little and James Brown, 1848. (originally 1680)

Jefferson, Thomas. *"Thomas Jefferson to J. (John Adams, 28 December 1812,"* Founders Online, National Archives. (re: Thomas Morton)

Jenks, Tudor. *Captain Myles Standish*. New York: The Century Co., 1905.

Jenness, John Scribner. *The Isles of Shoals, An Historical Sketch*. Boston: Houghton, Mifflin and Company, 1873.

_____. *Notes on the First Planting of New Hampshire and on the Piscataqua Patents*. Portsmouth: Lewis W. Brewster, 1878.

_____. *Transcripts of Original Documents in the English Archives Relating to the Early History of the State of New Hampshire*. New York: Privately Printed, 1876.

Johnson, Edward. *The Wonder-Working Providence of Sion's Savior in New England*. Andover: Warrn F. Draper, 1867. (originally 1654 with later introduction by William Fredrick Poole)

Josselyn, John. *Account of Two Voyages to New-England*. United Kingdom: Giles Widdowes, 1674.

Klein, Christopher. "The Real Story Behind Plymouth Rock." *History.com*

Kupperman, Karen Ordahl. "Thomas Morton, Historian." *The New England Quarterly* vol. 50, no. 4 (December, 1977): 660-664.

Lawry, Nelson. "Dover in 1623: Ssaith Who?" *Dover Times*, April 30, 1998.

Luedtke, Barbara E. *The Archaeology of Thompson Island*. Department of Anthropology, University of Massachusetts, August, 1996.

Lupher, David A. *Greeks, Romans, and Pilgrims: Classical Receptions in Early New England*. Leiden: Brill, 2017. (re: Thomas Morton)

MacInnes, C. M. *Ferdinando Gorges and New England*. The Bristol Branch of the Historical Association, 1965.

Major, Minor Wallace. "William Bradford versus Thomas Morton." *Early American Literature* 5, no. 2 (1970): 1–13.

Mancall, Peter C. *The Trials of Thomas Morton: an Anglican Lawyer, His Puritan Foes, and the Battle for a New England*. USA: Yale University Press, 2019.

Massachusetts Historical Society. *Collections of the Massachusetts Historical Society for the Year 1794.* Boston: Munroe & Francis, 1810, Archive.org

Maverick, Samuel. *A Brief Description of New England and the Several Towns Therein, Together with the Present Government Thereof.* Boston: Press of David Clark & Son, 1885. (originally 1660)

May, Ralph. *Early Portsmouth History.* Boston: C.E. Goodspeed & Co., 1926.

McClintock, John Norris. *History of New Hampshire: Colony, Province, State, 1623-1888.* Boston: B.B. Russell, 1889.

McIntyre, Ruth A. *Debts Hopeful and Desperate: Financing the Plymouth Colony.* Plymouth: Plimoth Plantation, 1963.

McPhee, John. "Travels of the Rock," *The Princeton Anthology of Writing: Favorite Pieces by the Ferris/McGraw Writers at Princeton University,* 2001.

McQuaid, Cate. "More Than Name Change May Be Needed at Former Plimoth Plantation," *Boston Globe,* November 19, 2020.

Molloy, Anne. *Captain Waymouth's Indians.* Hastings House, 1956. (fiction)

Moody, Edward C. *Handbook History of the Town of York, from Early Times to the Present.* Augusta: York Publishing Company, 1914.

Moody, Robert Earle. "A Re-Examination of the Antecedents of the Massachusetts Bay Company's Charter of 1629." *Proceedings of the Massachusetts Historical Society* 69 (1947): 56-498.

Morison, Elizabeth Forbes and Elting E. Morison. *New Hampshire: A Bicentennial History.* New York: W. W. Norton & Company, Inc., 1976.

Morison, Samuel Eliot. "The Plymouth Colony and Virginia." *The Virginia Magazine of History and Biography* vol. 62, no. 2 (April, 1954): 147-165.

Morton, Thomas and Francis Adams (editor). *The New English Canaan.* Boston: The Prince Society, 1883. (originally 1637)

Moses, J.M. "Pioneers of Little Harbor and Vicinity." *Granite Monthly,* vol. xlv, 1913.

Moulton, Augustus F. *Sir Ferdinando Gorges and His Palatinate of Maine, An Address*. Portland: Maine Historical Society and American Historical Society, 1903.

Murphy, Edith. "'A Rich Widow, Now to Be Tane Up or Laid Downe': Solving the Riddle of Thomas Morton's 'Rise Oedipeus.'" *The William and Mary Quarterly* 53, no. 4 (1996): 755–68.

Newcott, Bill. "400 Years On, the Pilgrims Get a Reality Check." *NationalGeographic.com*

Page, Elwin L. "A.D. 1623." *Granite Monthly* LIV (1923): 205-211.

Parsons, Langdon B. *History of the Town of Rye, NH*. Concord: Rumford Press, 1905.

Pearson, Tom. "First N.H. Settlers' Monument Being Returned to Its Home." *Rye Reflections*, April, 2007.

Philbrick, Nathaniel. *Mayflower: A Story of Courage, Community, and War*. New York, NY: Viking Press, 2006.

Piper, Doris Delaware. *Stories of Old New Hampshire*. Orford: Equity Publishing Company, 1963. (for children, illustrated by Alden Burt)

Poor, John Albert. *English Colonization in America. A Vindication of the Claims of Sir Ferdinando Gorges, as the Father of English Colonization in America (Delivered Before the Historical Society of Maine and New York)*. New York: D. Appleton & Co., 1862.

Pope, Charles Henry. *The Pioneers of Maine and New Hampshire, 1623 to 1660: A Descriptive List, Drawn from Records of the Colonies, Towns, Churches, Courts and other Contemporary Sources*. Boston: C.H. Pope, 1908.

Pory, John, Emmanuel Altham, and Isaack de Rasieres, Sydney V. James, Jr. (editor). *Three Visitors to Early Plymouth: Letters about the Pilgrim Settlement in New England During Its First Years*. Plimoth Plantation, Inc., 1963.

Potter, Chandler Eastman. *The Military History of the State of New-Hampshire, from Its Settlement, in 1623, to the Rebellion, in 1861*. Concord: McFarland & Jenks, 1868.

Pratt, Eleazer Franklin. *Phineas Pratt and Some of this Descendants*. Boston: Privately Printed, 1897. (includes Phineas Pratt's "A Declaration of the Affairs of the English People")

Preston, Richard A. "The :Laconia Company of 1629: an English Attempt to Intercept the Fur Trade." *Canadian Historical Review* vol. 31, no. 2 (June 1950): 125-144.

———. *Gorges of Plymouth Fort: A Life of Sir Ferdinando Gorges, Captain of Plymouth Fort, Governor of New England, and Lord of the Province of Maine*. United States: University of Toronto Press, 1953.

Quinn, David B. "Review of *A Life of Sir Ferdinando Gorges, Captain of Plymouth Fort, Governor of New England, and Lord of the Province of Maine*, by Richard Arthur Preston. *The Canadian Historical Review* vol. 36, no. 4 (1955): 349-351.

Quint, Alonzo H. *The First Parish in Dover, NH*. Dover: Printed for the Parish, 1884.

Robinson, J. Dennis. *Under the Isles of Shoals: Archaeology and Discovery on Smuttynose Island*. Portsmouth Marine Society Press, 2012.

———. *New Castle: New Hampshire's Oldest, Smallest, and Only Island Town*. Great Life Press. 2023.

———. Various articles published in the *Portsmouth Herald, Foster's Daily Democrat. New Hampshire Gazette, New Hampshire Magazine, SeacoastNH.com*, and elsewhere from 1997-2023.

Rose-Troup, Fraances. *Roger Conant and the Early Settlements on the North Shore of Massachusetts*. Roger Conant Family Association, Inc., 1926.

Rosier, James. *Rosier's Relation of Waymouth's Voyage to the Coast of Maine, 1605*. United States: GorgesSociety, 1887.

Sabine, Lorenzo. *Report on the Principal Fisheries of the American Seas* (Prepared for the U.S. Treasury Department). Washington, DC: Robert Armstrong, Printer, 1863.

Sanborn, Edwin David, Channing Harris Cox. *History of New Hampshire, from Its First Discovery to the Year 1830*. United States: J.B. Clarke, 1875.

Scales, John. *History of Dover, New Hampshire*. Dover: Printed by the Authority of the City Council, 1923.

Scott, Adrian and Henry A. Whitney. *The Thompson Family*. Uxbridge, MA: The Mendon Historical Society, 1913.

Shipton, Clifford K. *Roger Conant: A Founder of Massachusetts*. Cambridge, MA: Harvard University Press, 1944.

Smith, Daniel J. *Rambles About the Dover Area 1623-1973*. Hancock Press, 1973.

Smith, Captain John. *A Description of New England*. Rochester: George P. Humphrey, 1898 (1622 edition, originally 1616)

Snow, Edward Rowe. *The Romance of Boston Bay*. Boston: The Yankee Publishing Company, 1944.

Snow, Stephen Eddy. *Performing the Pilgrims. A Study of Ehtnohistorical Role-Playing at Plimoth Plantation*. Jackson: University of Mississippi, 1993.

Stackpole, Everett S. *Old Kittery and Her Families*. Lewiston, Maine: Press of Lewiston Journal Company, 1903.

———. *History of New Hampshire*. New York: The American Historical Society, 1916.

Stanley, Raymond W. *The Four Thompsons of Boston Harbor, 1621-1965*. Boston: Thompson Academy, 1966.

State Street Trust Company. *Towns of New England and Old England, Ireland and Scotland . . . Connecting Links Between Cities and Towns of New England and Those of the Same Name in England, Ireland and Scotland*. Boston: Walton Advertising & Printing Co., 1920.

Sumner, William Hyslop. *A History of East Boston, with Biographical Sketches of Its Early Proprietors*. Boston: J.E. Hilton and Company, 1858.

The Thompson Family Genealogy, https://freepages.rootsweb.com/~nivek/genealogy/

Thompson, Ralph E. and Matthew R. Thompson. *The First Yankee: David Thomson, 1592-1628*. Portsmouth, NH: Peter E. Randall, for the Piscataqua Pioneers, 1997.

———. *Pascataway, De Facto Capital of New England, 1623-1630.* Portsmouth, NH. (typed report, 58 pages)

Tomson Web Centre, wellswooster.com/tommies/

Trewlawny, Robert and James Phinney Baxter (editor). *The Trelawny Papers.* United States: Hoyt, Fogg, and Donham, 1884. (includes Amias Maverick's 1635 letter)

Tuttle, Charles Wesley, with John Ward Dean. *Capt. John Smith, Founder of New Hampshire.* Boston: The Prince Society, 1887.

Van Deventer, David E. *The Emergence of Provincial New Hampshire, 1623-1741.* Bowie, MD: Heritage Books, 1996.

Wadleigh, George. *Notable Events in the History of Dover, New Hampshire: From the First Settlement in 1623 to 1865.* Dover, NH: G.H. Wadleigh, 1913.

Walker, Joseph B. "The First Settlement of New Hampshire." *Granite Monthly* vol. 28 (1900): 56-58. (includes dedication speech of 1623 monument in Rye, NH)

Warren, Wendy. *New England Bound: Slavery and Colonization in Early America.* New York: W.W. Norton & Company, 2016.

———. "'The Cause of Her Grief': The Rape of a Slave in Early New England." *The Journal of American History* 93, no. 4 (2007): 1031–49. (re: Samuel Maverick)

Watts, Jenny Chamberlain, William Richard Cutter, Mellen Chamberlain. *A Documentary History of Chelsea: Including the Boston Precincts of Winnisimmet, Rumney Marsh, and Pullen Point, 1624-1824.* United States: Massachusetts Historical Society, 1908.

Whitbourne, Richard. *A Discourse Containing a Loving Invitation Both Honourable and Profitable to All Such as Shall Be Adventurers, Either in Person or Purse for the Advancement of His Majesties Most Hopefull Plantation in New-foundland, Lately Undertaken.* Imprinted at London by Felix Kyngston, 1622.

Whitehouse, Robert A. and Cathleen C. Beaudoin. *Ports of Dover: Two Centuries of Shipping on the Cochecho.* Portsmouth, NH: Portsmouth Marine Society, 1988.

Whiton, John Milton. *Sketches of the History of New-Hampshire, from Its Settlement in 1623, to 1833*. Concord: Marsh, Capen and Lyon, 1834.

Willison, George F. *Saints and Strangers*. New York: Reynal & Hitchcock, 1945.

Wilson, Ola Elizabeth. *Portsmouth, the Life of a Town*. New York: The MacMillan Company, 1966.

Winslow, Edward, Kelly Wisecup (editor). *Good News from New England (A Scholarly Edition)*. Boston: University of Massachusetts Press, 2014. (originally published in 1624)

——. (as Anonymous). *Mourt's Relation: A Journal of the Pilgrims in Plymouth*. United Kingdom: Applewood Books, 1986. (originally published 1647 in London)

Winsor, Justin. *Charles Deane, LLD, a Memoir. Privately Printed.* Cambridge: Press of John Wilson and Son, 1891.

Winthrop, John. *The Journal of John Winthrop, 1630-1649*. United Kingdom: Belknap Press of Harvard University Press, 2009. (first published in 1790 and 1825)

Young, Alexander. *Chronicles of the First Planters of the Colony of Massachusetts from 1623 to 1636*. Boston: Charles C. Little and James Brown, 1846.

Zuckerman, Michael. "Pilgrims in the Wilderness: Community, Modernity, and the Maypole at Merry Mount." *The New England Quarterly* vol. 50, no. 2 (June 1977): 255-277.

Places to Visit

For readers curious to see where the Thompsons lived, only two sites stand out. Both locations, coincidentally, offer outdoor environmental adventures for young people and their families.

Odiorne Point State Park in Rye, New Hampshire features sweeping views of the Gulf of Maine and Little Harbor, where Pannaway once stood. The park features diverse habitats, extensive walking trails, picnic areas, and a playground. Remnants of its rich social history remain throughout the park, from cellar holes of its grand estate years to its military defense occupation during World War II. The north end of the park features a public boat launch.

The Seacoast Science Center open year-round, provides educational experiences at Odiorne Point State Park on behalf of New Hampshire State Parks. An independent nonprofit institution, the Center features live-animal and interactive exhibits, hands-on enrichment programs, community science events, day camps, field trips, and much more. For more information visit seacoastsciencecenter.org.

The Thompson Island Outward Bound Education Center grew out of a unique 1833 program to create a natural sanctuary from city life in the heart of Boston, Massachusetts. For nearly 200 years, Thompson Island has been igniting a love of learning in students of all ages through experiential education. The island is also accessible via a scenic 25-minute ferry ride across Boston Harbor for family, wedding, and corporate events. Visit thompsonisland.org online for details.

About the Illustrations

From the author's collection of vintage images, listed here as they appear in the book.

A 1972 re-enactment of the 1621 "thanksgiving" at Plimoth Plantation outdoor museum in Plymouth, Massachusetts.

Mayflower II, a full-scale reproduction of the original Pilgrim ship, was built in Brixham, Devon, England. It arrived at Plymouth Harbor in June 1957 and is owned by Plimoth-Patuxet Museums.

Satirical illustration of a seventeenth-century apothecary constructed from his remedies and equipment by the French artist Nicolas de l'Armessin II.

A scene from Henry W. Longfellow's epic poem "The Courtship of Miles Standish" by Newell Convers Wyeth. The dramatic painting inaccurately represents the Wessagusset Massacre of 1623 that took place indoors when Standish suddenly attacked and killed Native warriors while they were seated at what was supposed to be a peaceful negotiation.

Detail from an early map of Boston Harbor with Thompson Island seen toward the bottom of the page.

A fisherman hauls in a large cod in this 1940s shot from ACME Newspictures.

A sixteen-year old descendant of Miles Standish stands at the supposed departure site of the original *Mayflower* in Plymouth, England as part of the 1950s Mayflower Project.

A 1950s newspaper photograph detailing the mast and rigging of the *Mayflower II*.

About the Author

J. Dennis Robinson is the author of sixteen books and over 3,000 published articles (so far) about history and culture. He lives in New Hampshire by the swirling Piscataqua River and can see a hint of Maine from his kitchen window. For more on his work—past, present, and in-progress, visit jdennisrobinson.com online.

.

Printed in Great Britain
by Amazon

8cab3abf-08d1-41f7-81cb-4e08d11711d3R01